Praise for *Walk and Talk Therapy*

"*Walk and Talk Therapy* is an honest and personal sharing of Jennifer Udler's expertise and experience about leveraging the power of nature as a partner in therapy. Udler's storytelling and humor makes for a fun and entertaining learning experience. Bravo!"

—**Robert Zarr, MD, MPH,** certified nature and forest
therapy guide and founder of Park Rx America

"Jennifer Udler has created a useful guide to walking therapy for practicing clinicians. I have found it helpful, and I recommend it to others who are interested in charting their own path on this exciting modality."

—**Thomas Doherty, PsyD,** past president of the Society for
Environmental, Population and Conservation Psychology
and founding editor of the academic journal *Ecopsychology*

"When most of us think of therapy, we picture it taking place in an office that probably includes a couch. But as Jen Udler's fantastic new book shows us, it doesn't have to be this way! *Walk and Talk Therapy* shows us how the therapeutic experience can be transformed by taking things outside and getting ourselves moving. By combining traditional therapy with the life-changing benefits of being in nature and moving our bodies, we can take things to the next level and help people live happier, healthier lives. Best of all, this gem of a book combines inspiring client stories with practical advice on how to incorporate walking and nature into therapy."

—**Jonah Paquette, PsyD,** author of *Happily Even After,*
Awestruck, and *The Happiness Toolbox*

"Jennifer Udler breathes new meaning into Ram Dass's words, 'We're all just walking each other home.' I'll take my therapy infused with movement and nature, the greatest healer of all. Let *Walk and Talk Therapy*—a well-researched, wise, compassionate, and experiential guide—safely move your practice outdoors."

—**Amy Weintraub,** yoga therapist and author of *Yoga for Depression,*
Yoga Skills for Therapists, and *Yoga for Your Mood Deck*

"This is the book many therapists, counselors, and psychological practitioners have long been waiting for! Decades of research studies have proven the healing benefits of a wide variety of nature-connection practices for various mental health challenges, but there still hasn't been enough specific guidance for clinicians regarding ethics, safety, confidentiality, note-taking, and unpredictable weather. Our mental health professional associations have been *way* too slow in addressing the ecotherapy clinical issues that would allow practitioners to take advantage of the huge healing benefits offered by the wide variety of ecopsychological protocols now backed by research. Ecopsychotherapists remain concerned about how to practice without running into roadblocks from legal, insurance, or agency concerns. So this book is greatly needed. After all, even Sigmund Freud himself practiced walk and talk therapy (and included his dog Jofi in therapy sessions)! Thanks to Jen Udler and her inspiring book, mental health practitioners can now enjoy savvy guidance on how we too can enjoy the benefits of nature-based therapies."

—**Linda Buzzell, LMFT,** coeditor of *Ecotherapy: Healing with Nature in Mind*

"*Walk and Talk Therapy* brings academic research, therapeutic wisdom, practical information, and common sense to the practice of delivering mental health services while moving the body. Jennifer Udler draws on clinical experience and creativity, along with a personal love of walking, to persuade the reader to get out of their office and onto the trail! Many clients will benefit from this approach."

—**Britt Rathbone, LCSW-C,** adolescent therapist, trainer, and author

"What a fabulous guide to taking therapy work outside! Jennifer Udler weaves practical guidance together with clinical examples to show you how you could make walk and talk therapy a part of your work. Studies show that being in natural environments and bilateral movement (like walking) can greatly increase the brain and body's resilience and integration capacities. I was so glad to see Jennifer guide us through seasons of walking with clients, and she covers the concerns that so often come up around confidentiality and care needs that are different in public spaces where we might do our walk and talk work. We are told in school to meet clients where they are. This book shows us how to help clients access therapy in a way that works for them. A must-read for anyone who already engages in walk and talk therapy or who has even contemplated adding it to their work for their own health as well as for their clients' well-being."

—**Juliane Taylor Shore, LMFT, LPC, SEP**

"Jen Udler's new book about her walk and talk practice will inform therapists about this innovative approach that recognizes the importance of movement along with clinical conversation. She backs up her longtime commitment to walking and talking with clients with a compendium of ideas that details the whys and hows along with informative case examples. *Walk and Talk Therapy* will be a valuable tool for creative therapists considering an out-of-the-box approach to enhance their practice."

—**Michael Kerman, MSW,** founder of Leading Edge Seminars Inc.

"I found Jennifer Udler's writing style delightful and well-informed. It was like a Sunday morning coffee with a really good friend. Jennifer fills a niche for those wanting to expand or pivot their practice into nature or for those wanting to get their providers outside. Reading through *Walk and Talk Therapy*, I kept thinking this is a great author that is definitely on the right path."

—**David Sabgir, MD FACC,** CEO of Walk with a Doc

Walk and Talk Therapy

A Clinician's Guide to Incorporating Movement and Nature into Your Practice

Jennifer Udler, LCSW-C

Walk and Talk Therapy
Copyright © 2023 by Jennifer Udler
Published by
PESI Publishing, Inc.
3839 White Ave
Eau Claire, WI 54703

Cover and interior design by Amy Rubenzer
Editing by Chelsea Thompson

ISBN: 9781683736448 (print)
ISBN: 9781683736462 (ePDF)
ISBN: 9781683736455 (ePUB)

PESI Publishing
pesipublishing.com

This book is for my parents, Eileen and Fred Wolpert, who instilled in me at a young age an appreciation for the beauty of the natural world and the connections that can be created on long walks.

“ *Come forth into the light of things, let nature be your teacher.* **”**

–William Wordsworth

Table of Contents

> **"** *Life is a journey,*
> *not a destination.* **"**
>
> *–Ralph Waldo Emerson*

Introduction

Welcome to this book and to the concept of walk and talk therapy!

I have been committed to using this therapeutic model with my clients since 2013. Back then, there was no official class or list of best practices to help me get started. Instead, I've developed my practice through the rewarding progress I've seen clients make, the growing pains I've experienced along the way, and the conversations I've had with other therapists over the years. As interest in walking therapy continues to grow throughout the country, I've done my best to craft the guidebook I wish I'd had when I was getting started.

Maybe you picked up this book because you realized that you have been *sitting* at your therapy job for way too long, and you are ready to move! Maybe you're the client, and you're thinking of giving this book to your therapist because you are interested in going outdoors to walk during your sessions. Maybe, just maybe, you are reading this because you are starting to think that the traditional office-based therapy model is only one of many ways to practice therapy.

No matter what your reasons might be, when you head out on the trail or mosey down the lane, I want it to be a positive experience that helps you get the most out of the therapy session. Not only can green space and repetitive motion help soothe and focus the patient, but these elements also provide a rich living metaphor for the topics and concerns that therapy seeks to address.

For example, as I sit down to write this introduction, the prospect of getting everything I want into this book gives me the feeling of approaching a tall mountain. The mountain represents all that I need to convey to you: experiences, lessons, ways to navigate, and more. While I'm eager to share everything I've learned about walk and talk with you, my excitement is already getting crowded by anxious thoughts about doing it justice—it's going to be quite a climb! Will I adequately explain how walk and talk therapy has improved the way I practice psychotherapy? Will I successfully communicate the stories that clients have shared while walking side by side with me over the past ten years? Most importantly, will you be inspired (and prepared) to explore walk and talk therapy for yourself? As I embark on writing this book, I keep my goal in mind: to look out from the mountain peak and not only understand how I made it here but also appreciate how every step has moved me forward. As so many adventurers have said, the journey matters as much as the destination.

A CHANGE OF PLAN

Growing up, I was never an athlete; instead, I was the kid whose shoe flew off during kickball. But after my third child was born, I felt the need to get my body back in shape. I first started running in 2010, starting with a mile and slowly building up my strength and stamina. This experience was nothing like the seventh-grade gym class "mandatory mile" (in which I'd finished last). This time around, I discovered that running offered a great relief, giving me time to myself and providing a place where I could reconnect with my body and regroup my scattered thoughts.

Still, participating in an actual race was never part of my plan. When a friend invited me to join her for an information session with the local road runners club, I just came along to keep her company. But to my own surprise, I ended up joining the First Time Marathon (FTM) group that year and made yet another discovery: The mental health benefits of my solo runs were amplified by group training. As we logged mile after mile, we chatted, encouraged each other, and even sang along to our playlists together. Over time, our interactions deepened—we'd talk about life challenges we were facing, ask each other for support, remind each other that we were strong and capable, and, yes, even talk about our feelings. It didn't escape my notice that all these interactions were very similar to those with my therapy clients every day. In both situations, we'd discuss thoughts, emotions, and strategies to cope.

Midway through training, we all received singlets that said *FTM: The journey is the reward; the marathon is the victory lap.* I already knew this idea to be true from my experience as a therapist—now I was learning it from an athletic perspective. That fall, after completing the Marine Corps Marathon in Washington, DC, I cried as I crossed the finish line at the Iwo Jima Memorial. The feeling of accomplishment, mixed with physical pain, was overwhelmingly emotional—it showed me how resilient I am like nothing ever had before.

The marathon training experience and its inspirational motto moved me to change the way that I worked with clients.

THERAPY, STEP BY STEP

After thirteen years as a traditional talk therapist, training for the marathon showed me how inherently therapeutic movement can be. My fellow runners were benefiting from moving and talking at the same time; could my clients also make greater progress if I made their sessions more active?

As excited as I was by this idea, I was also very nervous about moving therapy out of the safety of the office. I worried about weather concerns, confidentiality, and people not showing up. Despite these hesitations, in early 2013, I started quietly telling a few people about my idea for walking therapy. Within weeks, I signed up my very first outdoor client, a twelve-year-old boy with a history of depression and attention-deficit/hyperactivity disorder (ADHD). When I had previously seen him in my office, he was fidgety, uncomfortable, and slow to open up. But once we were out in nature, he was so at ease—"in his element," as his parents had said when I told them about my plan to move our sessions outside. While climbing rocks and exploring the woods that surrounded the trail, he talked openly and fluidly about the pressures of school, friends, family, and even his depression. We threw rocks and sticks into nearby streams as we discussed how it's okay to filter out the negativity in life and focus on what is helpful for him.

This client's positive experience gave me the confidence I needed to launch my new practice. Since then, I have seen hundreds of clients for "walk and talk" (as I call it), including children, adolescents, and adults. I've watched the combination of nature and movement work its healing magic on people who struggle with anxiety, depression, other mood-related disorders, ADHD, and obsessive-compulsive disorder (OCD); people who are facing challenges with self-injurious behaviors; people exploring their sexual identity; and people navigating trauma, divorce, relationship issues, grief, and loss. In ten years (and counting), I've yet to meet a client who doesn't feel a little better after working through their challenges one step on the nature trail at a time.

EVERYTHING YOU DIDN'T KNOW YOU NEEDED TO KNOW

Between my enthusiasm for walk and talk and the novelty of this therapy format, I've been consulted by many therapists who are just beginning to incorporate outdoor movement into their practice. One question I commonly receive is "Why can't I just start walking with my client? I have a lovely parking lot surrounded by trees right outside my office—there are only a few cars coming and going." While I commend these folks for their enthusiasm, there's a lot to learn before you throw open the doors of your office.

Another big question I am asked by fellow therapists is how much walking I do each week. I won't lie—it's a lot: ten miles per day on average! But that's entirely by choice—we'll discuss how to ease your way into the walk and talk format and find your personal "sweet spot" in chapter 14.

These questions (and all the others you didn't know you needed to ask) are the reason I wrote this book. While I wrote it primarily for professionals in the field of talk therapy (psychotherapists, psychologists, counselors, social workers, etc.), it's also meant for clients, patients, and anyone who wants to actively participate in their own therapeutic process. My goal is to present the many benefits of an outdoor, movement-based psychotherapy practice and provide the tools for you to develop your own system, from beginning a walk and talk practice to crafting a holistic sensory experience to aid your therapeutic work. I'll go over the big considerations therapists need to explore before heading outside, from foundational matters such as legal and safety concerns or how to preserve confidentiality in an open public setting, to practical considerations like timing, note taking, and the inherent unpredictability of the great outdoors. I'll also share a variety of stories from my own practice—from inspiring breakthrough moments to the humbling (and sometimes embarrassing) mistakes I've made—to help you in your own journey.

This book is broken down into four sections, each corresponding with a season of the year. I've chosen this structure because seasons offer a beautiful object lesson about adaptability in the face of change. Living on this planet means being subject to the forces of nature—we're not the same person in winter that we are in summer. As you read, you'll see how the time of year, with its unique weather and other outdoor conditions, may influence the moods and mindsets you encounter in your clients. You'll also see how each passing season can move us through life with a tangible sense of direction and meaning when we choose to pay attention.

Just this morning, I was walking with a client while she discussed her ongoing stress at work. Until today, she felt she had really made progress in this area. But recently, thanks to some new concerns that had just arisen, she'd begun berating herself for making mistakes, hit a low, and now felt upset about how she reacted.

As I paused for her words to settle, I looked around and allowed us both to notice the conditions of the March morning. Much of the ground around us was covered in snow, thanks to a surprise snowstorm over the weekend. Yet, while the temperatures hovered in the mid-thirties, we could see the advancement of spring in the sun, the chirping of birds, and the daffodils blooming, despite the cold. Seasons can be confusingly nonlinear, we agreed, sometimes taking one step forward and two steps back. Sounds a lot like life, doesn't it?

MOVING THERAPY FORWARD

The word from my marathon shirt that has always resonated with me most is *journey*. In the therapy world, *journey* is often synonymous with *process*, something we talk a lot about in sessions. Love, grief, change, dealing with trauma, learning how to cope with anxiety, depression, stress, and life's challenges—these are all unique processes (or journeys) that move us from point A to point B. Much like marathoners on a twenty-mile training run, we find ways to get through the discomfort and fatigue along the way. We share stories with friends, listen to music, use positive self-talk, and, yes, sometimes we cry. The more we engage with these practices, the more they empower us to overcome and even enjoy the challenges on our journey.

The beauty of walk and talk therapy is that it provides a living metaphor for how we move forward in any journey: one step at a time. (A metaphor, I might add, that I've found very successful in reaching people who would otherwise shy away from getting the mental health care they need.) While we rarely learn the "lessons" of therapy in one session, climbing to the top of a hill during that session offers instant proof that we are capable of enduring pain, that we can find ways to manage the pressures we face, and that pressing on toward our goals, even when our thoughts and feelings don't make it easy, is tremendously empowering. By experiencing and working through difficulties, we can build resiliency, a necessary trait in life. Even the part about the marathon being the victory lap applies: After doing the hard work, we all deserve joy in our lives.

A Note About Client Stories

When I began writing this book, I struggled with how to include my clients' stories while protecting their privacy. Without disclosing anything sensitive regarding our relationship or their experience in therapy, it's important to me to help readers visualize a walk and talk session by sharing the processes that take place in these sessions over time.

I communicated this to a number of clients, and I'm grateful to say that the overwhelming response was along the lines of: "Oh, that's great! I think walk and talk has been good for me—feel free to share my story." In the interest of transparency, I'll share with you what I told them about how case studies and client stories will be presented in this book:

1. I will be combining stories from a variety of clients in the narratives of this book's key "characters." In other words, all the stories in this book are true, but they didn't happen to the same person.

2. Not all of my current or past clients will be included in this book.

3. Every client's name, race, age, ethnicity, career, family details, and other identifying information have been changed to protect people's privacy. (If you are my client reading the book, it's possible you may identify some similarities to your situation. On the other hand, it's also possible that I have changed facts and details so much that you don't recognize your story.)

4. Again, these stories represent fragments of experiences, combined here for teaching purposes. What I hope to share with readers isn't the details of an individual client or session, but rather, the ideas that guide me through each session and the course that therapy takes as a result.

To my clients past and present: Thank you for helping me share walk and talk therapy with other practitioners and patients. I want you to know how honored I am that you chose me to share your stories, thoughts, and feelings. I am forever grateful that our paths have crossed and that you trust me to support you through your journey.

Sincerely,

Jennifer Udler, LCSW-C

Autumn:

Exploring the Abundance of Outdoor
Walk and Talk Therapy

> " *I will not follow where the path may lead, but I will go where there is no path, and I will leave a trail.* "

—Muriel Strode

Chapter 1

Beginning the Practice

When I first decided to move my therapy practice outside, I did exactly three things to set up my new offering:

- I decided on a name for the practice: *Positive Strides*.
- I printed business cards.
- I set up a bank account.

Here are the things I did *not* do:

- Research anything about walking therapy.
- Tell any other professionals about my out-of-the-box idea.
- Call my malpractice insurance, my licensing board, or a lawyer.

As I mentioned in the introduction, I was lucky to have a great first session with the twelve-year-old client. No injuries, no accidental run-ins with people who knew either of us, and the parents were happy with the experience. However, even the success of that first session wasn't enough to silence all the what-ifs that came flooding in. Whether it was my productive anxiety talking, or the litigious culture in which we live, I felt compelled to seek a better foundation for my practice.

The problem was where to find that foundation. Back in 2013, I had never come across any therapists doing sessions outdoors. Telehealth was barely a thing at that point, having just been greenlighted by the FDA, and while there were activity-based therapy models for certain issues (like wilderness programs for teens or yoga for trauma patients), talk therapy was relegated to an indoor office. Not only had I never seen such an idea discussed in graduate school or continuing education, but

I had never even heard another therapist mention it as a possibility. In fact, at one social service agency where I previously worked, psychotherapists were explicitly told to stay indoors with the client for the sake of everyone's safety, security, and liability.

Despite the success of my first seat-of-the-pants session, putting real thought into this new therapy model triggered a tidal wave of reservations and uncertainties in my mind. I've listed many of them below, from the theoretical to the practical—do any of them resonate with you?

- Doesn't the "therapeutic frame" include an office with chairs or sofas? If I take a client outside, will I be breaking the rules?

- Will my license and malpractice insurance cover this format of therapy? Or worse, could I lose my license or get sued?

- Will I be compromising my client's confidentiality if we are seen together during an outdoor session?

- What defines "best practices" in walking therapy?

- If my client becomes emotional or feels out of control, what will I do? Will I be able to handle that in the middle of a trail?

- What will happen if my client gets injured? Will I be to blame?

- Is this ethical? Is it responsible? Is it even safe?

- Last but not least, what about my own safety? (So typical of those in the helping professions to think of themselves last!)

With nothing but my own questions to guide me, I dug in and began to research, starting with my state licensing board. The responses I received to my many calls and emails were very . . . indifferent. The board neither condemned nor condoned the practice of outdoor walking therapy sessions—in fact, they did not say anything specific about it at all. Whether they did not know the answers or did not care, they didn't try to stop me.

With no guidance from my board, I thought back to the community-based interventions involved in my very first job as a social worker and case manager. We would frequently venture outside the office with clients who struggled with issues like developmental disabilities and serious mental illness. To help these clients practice life skills, we might walk around the neighborhood with them or support them in ordering a sandwich from a deli. Since our goal was to help them become more familiar with navigating everyday community settings, it only made sense that some experiences were more valuable and meaningful outside of an office. That memory was enough to convince me that this walk and talk thing was kosher!

Next, I googled the term "walking therapy," which led me to "walk and talk therapy," which in turn led to "outdoor therapy," "wilderness therapy," and "adventure therapy," which finally led me to people! To my surprise, just one walk and talk Facebook group included over 1,000 clinicians who practice walk and talk therapy in the U.S. alone. I discovered colleagues in California, Colorado, Minnesota, Texas, and beyond who were walking with clients on beaches, mountain trails, lakeside paths, and even greenways through the heart of major metropolitan areas.

I also discovered academic research (which I will get into in chapters 5 and 6) validating the benefits of walk and talk, though the number of practitioners was far greater than the amount of published data on the topic. Most of what I found consisted of articles supporting the case for increased exercise and green space to help improve people's overall mental health. Still, there was *just* enough science to encourage me that I was on the path to something legit.

At that point, I hadn't told any of my colleagues, supervisors, or even friends about my new outdoor-based practice. Being a therapist, I couldn't help but question what was driving my reluctance. Was it fear of being judged? Was it discomfort with changing the conventional methodology? Was it the worry that came with having no idea what I was doing and knowing that more work lay ahead of me? Yes, to all the above.

This realization motivated me to directly address my fears and vulnerabilities. First, I prepared answers to every question I could anticipate being asked by colleagues. Next, I began to talk about my proposed new practice with my support system of trusted friends. Finally, I took a hard look at all the legal and ethical variables my new practice posed, and I created a to-do list that included the following:

- Speak with a lawyer about liability and professional risk.

- Draft a new informed consent form to address issues of confidentiality and personal injury.

- Call my malpractice company and ask a ton of questions.

- Draft a safety plan for myself.

- Draft a list of safety precautions for clients.

- Look at other movement-based practices (yoga therapy, dance therapy, community-based therapeutic programs) to see how they handle personal injury liability.

- Enroll in multiple classes with my local Women's Business Center, where I learned all about business-related details I hadn't studied in graduate school for social work.

- Write a business plan and work on financial spreadsheets.

- Set up an LLC to protect me from personal liabilities.

- Build and launch a website for my revamped practice.

Once I did the work to set my practice on solid ground, I felt a lot more comfortable sharing the news about Positive Strides, LLC. I still remember the day I told my colleagues about my pivot to walk and talk. Good thing I braced myself—the reactions were all over the place!

- "So happy for you—that's so cool. Do you need any extra therapists? I love walking outside." (*Um, no thanks—I only have one client so far!*)

- "What about confidentiality? Will your clients feel comfortable meeting you with other people around in the park?" (*I'll start with an honest conversation with clients, backed up by my new informed consent.*)

- "Will you also have an office for rainy days?" (*No, that's what raincoats and umbrellas are for.*)

- "This will be great for teens! Let me know when you're ready to see one of my kids!" (*I may not be practicing in an office, but I still have boundaries, people!*)

Overall, I felt very supported by my colleagues. Even their (mostly) valid questions involved recognition of how this therapy model could work really well for some clients. Maybe the biggest boost to my confidence came when my longtime supervisor referred to my new practice with the endearing nickname "Happy Feet!" Thanks to everyone's support, I felt officially ready to hang up my shingle and open the doors.

LEARNING AS WE GO

With my walk and talk practice officially launched, the next order of business was to find more clients to walk and talk with. I laced up my sneakers, got out my freshly printed business cards, and began pounding the pavement. I set up meetings with anyone who was interested: therapists, psychiatrists, pediatricians, school counselors. Nearly all were very open to the idea of walk and talk, though I did encounter a naysayer or two. I remember meeting with one doctor who said, "I can't picture it. What happens when someone has to walk in front and someone behind on a trail? I love to sit and face my therapist for the whole session—it is very deep and gratifying for me to make direct eye contact with her." I responded that not everyone loves direct face-to-face interaction as much as she does; still, needless to say, I did not receive any client referrals from her.

I'd expected some pushback from colleagues, but one thing I did not anticipate was that some clients would prove to be more comfortable around pavement than a dirt trail, like the adult male client who, for some reason, chose to try walk and talk despite having a deep fear of spiders and overgrown vines (which he did not tell me about). His fears proved to be a bit of a stumbling block in our first few sessions; however, walking therapy ultimately offered us an opportunity to work through them together.

I also hadn't anticipated how social identity would factor into this therapy format. Although I have always lived and worked in very diverse neighborhoods, not all clients are comfortable walking with a White woman in public settings. I have had some honest and sometimes uncomfortable conversations with Black clients about what it's like for them to stroll through the park with me. Even here, the discomfort led to opportunity— exploring the raw emotions surrounding race, ethnicity, and other social factors brought out a different aspect of the therapeutic relationship and offered insight into my clients' lives.

In hindsight, the things that I did *not* initially do, as well as the things that I did instinctively, helped lay the foundation for the practice I have today. We all learn from both our positive successes and the mistakes we make; the nuances we uncover allow our practices to evolve. We'll get into those nuances in more detail later in the book; for now, the big-picture question we want to answer is, what makes walk and talk work? If what you've read so far has your brain stewing and your feet itching, let's get started!

Chapter 2

Why Practice Therapy This Way?

It's mid-October, and I am sitting on a park bench waiting for my new client Jake to arrive. The sun is shining, there's a cool breeze, and I'm surrounded by an autumnal rainbow of trees nearing their seasonal peak.

Jake called a few days ago after seeing my card on a bulletin board at the YMCA. He said that he had never considered counseling before, but when he saw that he could walk and be in therapy at the same time, he was curious. Jake had just suffered a massive loss—his wife of twenty years died only six months earlier. Not only was he was feeling heartbroken, he told me on the phone, but raising two teenage children on his own had made life overwhelming for him.

From my bench, I see a White man in his late forties pull up, park, and approach me.

"Jen?" he calls.

"Yes! Jake? Very nice to meet you!"

We smile and shake hands.

"If you're ready," I say, "we can head out on the path this way."

We walk side by side on a wide, paved path that runs through the woods, along streams, and over small bridges. After a brief chat about the gorgeous fall weather, I start the conversation.

"I know we spoke a bit on the phone about why you contacted me, but can you tell me a little more, now that we are together in person?"

"Yes . . ." Jake hesitates a bit. "You know, my family, we never saw therapists. It's not something we did. We relied on each other, or we just didn't talk about things."

He laughs a little nervously. I nod encouragingly—it's not the first time I've heard this from a client.

Jake continues, "I have always turned toward swimming or running to deal with my emotions or stressful events in life. Since my wife died, I have continued to run, and that has been helpful. However, I am beginning to think that it's not quite enough. So when I saw your card, I felt like I might be comfortable with this type of counseling."

Since it is often helpful to warm up with a topic that the client is comfortable discussing, I ask Jake to tell me more about his exercise routine.

"I swim on the weekends at the Y, and I go out every morning for a four-mile jog. It's my quiet time to just think, before the kids get up and the routine of the day begins. The everyday stuff is when I really feel the loss of my wife. She used to be in the kitchen when I got back from my morning runs. We would talk, have coffee, and make lunches for the kids."

Jake pauses for a deep breath but keeps walking at the same brisk pace.

I respond, "This is really hard. I can see how painful your loss is. I want you to know that this is a safe place to talk about it. We will go at your pace, both emotionally and in our walks."

"Thank you" he says, and I can see his eyes begin to mist up. He takes another deep breath. "I think I really need this."

· · · · ·

Doing our jobs as therapists means focusing on the needs of the individual client. We meet the client where they are, make sense of and bring awareness to their emotions, and find (or invent) ways to help them reach their goals. Beginning my career as a social worker introduced me early on to working with clients in non-office settings. I remember eye-opening home visits that allowed me deep insight into the real lifestyles and daily experiences of my clients. School social work offered a similar opportunity to see clients in their own environment, whether it was observing a child's behavior in the classroom or searching the building to find a kid's secret hiding spot for avoiding his classes.

Community interventions aren't uncommon for private practice therapists, either. One therapist I know regularly takes his clients to a coffee shop to desensitize them to uncomfortable social situations. They order a drink, sit in the café, maybe even practice speaking to strangers. Another therapist who practices exposure therapy with clients with OCD will have them go into the nearby shopping center to touch doorknobs, pick up fruit, and then eat a snack, all without engaging in ritualistic behaviors.

At the heart of these interventions is compassionate creativity—we're looking for ways to make therapy effective, accessible, and inviting for people who may not otherwise engage with it. Walk and talk is a new outgrowth of this creativity, and not just for athletes or outdoor enthusiasts. Some of my most dedicated walk and talk clients are decidedly "indoor" types whose sneakers otherwise live in the back of the closet. Some are elderly folks; some have limited mobility. In other words, walk and talk isn't about going far or fast, any more than art therapy is about producing a gallery-worthy painting. The point isn't that it's therapy with a workout on the side; rather, it's harnessing the mind-body connection in ways that serve a client's unique needs. While it can feel a bit daunting to shake up the tried-and-true therapy model that most of us have been trained to follow, I offer you a quick overview of the benefits that keep my walk and talk clients coming back for more:

- **Expanding access to therapy.** For clients who are intimidated by the traditional office setting, the constant movement and lack of eye contact in walk and talk can be a more comfortable context for easing into the therapeutic conversation.

- **Giving clients a choice.** Walk and talk offers a choice for clients to experience another type of physical and emotional space. Simply having this choice can be deeply empowering, even before the benefits of nature and movement kick in.

- **Walking is freeing.** Research shows that movement facilitates the release of emotions. When someone is overwhelmed with worry, moving can decrease both physical and mental stress.

- **Increasing mind-body awareness.** Actively moving while discussing feelings can help to unpack the bodily sensations of repressed emotions.

- **Increasing confidence, especially regarding the body.** People who suffer from low self-esteem or a poor body image may feel better about themselves while being active, thus providing more confidence to share feelings.

- **Empowering the therapist do their best work.** Last but certainly not least, walk and talk offers myriad benefits to the therapist! Combining a session with outdoor movement can encourage the therapist to be more comfortable, creative, and alert, making them a more effective practitioner.

The longer I've practiced walk and talk, the better I've become at identifying clients who would benefit from it or who have specific concerns that outdoor movement can help uniquely address.

Jake is a prime walk and talk therapy candidate for several reasons:

- He is familiar and comfortable with outdoor activity.

- He has no experience with or exposure to therapy.

- Having suffered a major loss in his life, he recognized his own need for support and was motivated enough to do something about it.

That last point is particularly important. While we are still battling a widespread stigma around mental health care in our culture, there has been a very positive trend of open dialogue about mental health issues. Leaders in entertainment, media, sports, and popular culture seem increasingly willing to discuss their mental health struggles, share the ways they have found support, and even provide access to on-site counseling. Just this past year, two Olympic athletes not only openly presented their struggles with depression and anxiety to the world, but even had the bravery and inner strength to prioritize their well-being over their athletic careers. Meanwhile, adolescents and young adults are much more likely to share candidly that they are in therapy or on medication for mental health challenges. There are mental health organizations in high schools, mental wellness days on college campuses, and even a national Mental Health Awareness month observed here in the U.S. (It's the month of May, for those wondering.) Thanks to this positive momentum, some populations are turning a corner in their recognition of the importance of mental health and the power and freedom that come from seeking support.

While walking therapy has been around for a lot longer than you might realize (we'll discuss its origins later in the book), the significant progress in destigmatizing mental health care has paved the way for walk and talk to thrive. When I ask clients how they feel about walking outside with me, their responses often include an element of pride that they are in therapy, working on themselves, and overcoming the issues that used to hold them back. As a result, they are neither ashamed nor embarrassed to be seen with their therapist. As one client expressed it, "I go to the dentist, the doctor, and therapy. When I go to the doctor, I almost always see someone I know in the waiting room. I'm not embarrassed about that, so why would I care if someone saw me with my therapist?" This is the change that the mental health care community has been working so hard to achieve. We have come a long way from the days of institutionalization, secrecy, and shame—let's keep marching forward.

Chapter 3

What Is Walking Therapy?

Now that we understand more about why walking therapy is such a valuable option for clients (and therapists, too), let's answer some basic questions about what walking therapy entails. It's really as simple and intuitive as breaking down the three elements within the practice: walking, nature, and therapy.

WALKING

There is an abundance of research that confirms the positive relationship between exercise and mental health. Diverse forms of movement have been used to effectively treat a variety of mental health concerns, including anxiety, depression, ADHD, bereavement, post-traumatic stress, and other life stressors. Moving our bodies feels good (especially when our minds and emotions are down) and also opens up possibilities to foster a growth mindset. In *The Body Keeps the Score*, pioneering trauma researcher Dr. Bessel van der Kolk (2014) writes:

> *In contrast to the Western reliance on drugs and verbal therapies, other traditions from around the world rely on mindfulness, movement, rhythms, and action. Yoga in India, tai chi and qigong in China, and rhythmical drumming throughout Africa are just a few examples. The cultures of Japan and the Korean peninsula have spawned martial arts, which focus on the cultivation of purposeful movement and being centered in the present, abilities that are damaged in traumatized individuals. . . . These techniques all involve physical movement, breathing, and meditation. (pp. 209–210)*

Since van der Kolk's work was published, many forms of movement-based therapy have been developed and practiced with great success for client outcomes. So why have I chosen to focus my practice on the simplest form of movement? Exactly *because* it's simple! Walking requires no training or special equipment, making it widely accessible for most patients and easily adaptable to those who use wheelchairs or assistive devices. But that's not the only feature that makes walking an ideal form of therapeutic movement:

- **Walking gets our thoughts "unstuck."** Along with the physical release of endorphins and other hormones that make us feel good and decrease unhealthy thoughts and behaviors, the physical act of moving forward seems to trigger a mental movement toward open-mindedness. Whenever I'm walking with clients, a certain rhythm and ease sets into the therapy session. This may be the result of bilateral stimulation, a technique often employed in somatic therapies such as eye movement desensitization and reprocessing (EMDR). The more we integrate functions from both sides of the brain—such as walking and talking at the same time—the more we're able to loosen up our thought patterns and consider new approaches to old problems.

- **Walking is fundamental to who we are as a species.** Humans began walking approximately five million years ago, about two million years prior to our brain growth, and we are still the only animals on this planet to walk upright. As humans, walking is wired into our survival. The draw we feel to climb a hill or reach a body of water is more than just our eagerness for a scenic view—it's an echo of our ancient ancestors' search for strategic positions that would help sustain life.

- **Walking cultivates connection.** Now more than ever, we humans need a sense of belonging and purpose. When we walk and talk with another person, we reassure our brains that we are safe, wanted, and not alone. It's interesting to note that walking is deeply integrated in religious practices and historical and cultural movements around the world: Muslims taking a pilgrimage to Mecca, Christians hiking el Camino de Santiago in Spain, Jews forgoing their vehicles to walk with their families to synagogue as part of their Sabbath observance, even nonreligious people finding meaning and sometimes spiritual transformation while hiking the Appalachian Trail or another awe-inspiring pathway. There is also a long history of activists and organizers bringing supporters together for mass marches that demonstrate their power in unity. Over the years, my friends and I have participated in walks to raise awareness about a wide range of concerns, including hunger, homelessness, racism, misogyny, breast cancer, suicide, domestic violence, and opioid addiction. When we walk together, we foster a sense of meaningful community in moving forward.

NATURE

I often refer to nature as my co-therapist. Just being in nature is shown to calm the nervous system, as many cultures and ethnic groups around the world have demonstrated through nature-centered traditions and rituals. The growing fields of ecopsychology and ecotherapy explore the healing that happens when a person reconnects their sense of self with the natural world around them, a connection known in scientific circles as *biophilia*. As author Florence Williams (2017) writes in her book *The Nature Fix*, "The biophilia hypothesis posits that peaceful or nurturing elements of nature helped us regain equanimity, cognitive clarity, empathy, and hope. . . . Biophilia explains why even today we build houses on the lake, why every child wants a teddy bear, and why Apple names itself after a fruit" (p. 22).

We'll get deeper into the research behind this phenomenon in chapter 5, but for now, here are just a few of the documented mental health benefits of spending time outdoors:

- **Seeing green space improves mood and decreases anxiety.** "Green exercise," another term for exercising outdoors, has been shown to improve both self-esteem and mood. According to a 2010 study (Barton & Pretty, 2010), all participants benefited from exercising outdoors, and those with views of water had an even greater improvement in mood. Interestingly, those with existing mental health diagnoses had some of the greatest improvements in self-esteem. Additionally, exercising outdoors gives our minds a break, and with no specific focus coupled with being in a restorative space, stress levels go down (Gladwell et al., 2013).

- **Exposure to sunlight is a natural mood lifter.** Spending the majority of our time indoors reduces our intake of ultraviolet B rays, which are critical for our bodies to manufacture the mood-regulating hormone vitamin D. More outdoor time means more D, which means improved symptoms of depression and other mood disorders.

- **Spending time in nature reduces stress.** Numerous studies since the 1980s have documented how time in nature triggers a reduction in cortisol, blood pressure, and other physical markers of stress, as well as a quicker recovery time after stressful events.

- **Nature enhances creativity.** Have you ever been stuck while working on a project and stepped outside to get some fresh air? Thanks to all the factors we just reviewed, nature has a special way of helping you think about problems in new ways, leading to unexpected solutions. This boosted creativity is of great use in therapy—taking patients outdoors can help them see the issues they're facing with a fresh perspective.

THERAPY

I'm often asked what kind of therapeutic techniques can be used during walking sessions. The answer is almost any! Just about any modality you're currently using in your practice can also be used during walk and talk—it's just a matter of creatively adapting them to your new outdoor venue. I find that therapeutic interventions become memorable illustrations in outdoor sessions. Metaphors drawn from the scenery around us (such as paths, streams, or bridges) can often reinforce the discussion and lead to impactful growth.

Let's take a closer look at how some common therapeutic approaches can be easily adapted for use in outdoor sessions.

MINDFULNESS

Mindfulness is all about bringing awareness to the feelings and to the moment in which they occur. As therapists, we guide our clients to a place of *allowing* feelings to happen and inviting compassionate exploration of the thoughts that accompany them. We then bring physical awareness to blend with the emotions, asking our clients to identify where they feel it in their bodies. The goal is to encourage a connection between mind and body that can help clients relax enough to get in touch with themselves and articulate what they're feeling.

> *I want to note here that people sometimes use motion or activity as a way to distract themselves from feeling difficult things. Surprisingly, walk and talk can be precisely what helps these people ease into a greater sense of awareness. Rather than using the movement to avoid uncomfortable feelings, we use the movement to engage them. The goal is to settle into peace, stillness, and acceptance of difficult feelings.*

Most mindfulness exercises can be done while walking; some are even more conducive when walking, as the act of engaging the body increases the client's awareness.

Sometimes I begin a session with a very simple mindfulness exercise to help the client clear their head and get grounded in the present so that they're able to focus on our time together. Other times, I'll use a mindfulness meditation in the middle of a session to help the client feel more stable after becoming overwhelmed with emotion. Sometimes it's as simple as practicing being present and aware of a situation without reacting, allowing us time to reflect and make a sharper decision for how to proceed. There's no rule as to which mindfulness exercise is "best"—I always go with the one that seems right at the time, then follow up by asking, "What do you notice?"

Here are a few examples of how I've incorporated some classic mindfulness exercises into walk and talk sessions:

- **Noticing each of the five senses.** I invite the client to name what they see, hear, smell, taste, and touch. The colors and depth of view provide myriad choices for the client while practicing this exercise.

- **Appreciating the change in seasons.** I ask the client to identify some of the signs of the season we are in or transitioning into. Slowing down and noticing a golden leaf at the end of summer can bring a keen sense of awareness of an upcoming transition.

- **Taking a moment to notice what is going on around you.** I prompt the client to pause and describe any action they observe around us. Wooded trails are great for this!

- **Basic body scan.** I guide the client in bringing awareness to each section of their body, from head to toe. This is a particularly great exercise for a nature trail, especially with the help of a light breeze or a patch of sunlight falling through the trees.

- **Breathing exercises.** I lead the client in some simple breathwork practices—a few of my favorites include triangle breathing (inhale for a count of four, hold four, exhale four), ujjayi or oceanic breathing (synchronized with body movements), and alternate nostril breathing (looks just how it sounds).

Wondering how this works in practice? The following is a real-life story that shows how I incorporated mindfulness therapy into a walk and talk session.

• • • • •

Joanie is a twenty-five-year-old White woman who self-identifies as gay and queer. Though she has a job and lives on her own, she stated that when it comes to "adulting," she feels like she has no idea what she's doing. In her first session, she tells me about a time when she went to a friend's house for a party but panicked after ten minutes and left without saying goodbye; this leads to her sharing her history with anxiety and ADHD, and her desire to address some issues related to her sense of self.

During our second session together, Joanie seems ready to open up about her reasons for wanting to talk to a therapist. About halfway through our trail walk, she tells me, "I can't even sit down while I'm eating. I have realized that for the past three days, I have eaten all of my meals standing up."

"What's that like for you?" I ask.

"I just can't seem to relax. When I'm supposed to be relaxing, I only hear myself telling myself to relax, never really achieving the goal of relaxing."

"Aha, I get it. You feel revved up, ready to move, yet you want to relax, if only . . ."

"Exactly," Joanie breaks in. "Sometimes I don't even feel like I am where I am."

At precisely that moment, we emerge from the wooded trail. The clearing ahead of us offers a view of a hilly field of grass, surrounded by bushes and small trees starting to show the colors of early fall.

"Joanie," I say, "let's stop here a minute." To be honest, I'm a little worried she won't feel comfortable standing still—she's really been on a roll! But she easily lets the walk and the conversation come to a pause.

"Can you put one hand on your belly and one on your upper chest, and feel yourself breathing?" She does. "Now, can you take a deeper breath in through your nose, and a long exhale out through your nose?"

We do this together, repeating it four more times.

"Okay, now what do you notice?" I ask.

Up to this point, I've only seen Joanie when she is "buzzing"—I'm amazed by how still she becomes while doing this exercise. She radiates calm as she says, "I see those yellow leaves on the tree over there. They stand out from the green, and they look really nice."

I give her an encouraging "Yes!" in response, then ask her to do the same breathing exercise, but this time saying "I am" on the inhale and "here" on the exhale. At first, she breathes and says the words out loud and quickly: "I am. Here." I ask her to say the words inside her head, slowly, two more times, and I focus on my own breath as I wait by her side.

When she completes her second exhale, I ask again, "What do you feel now?"

She thoughtfully responds, "I feel present. I feel calm. I am grounded, and I am only thinking about being here right now. Nothing else."

"Yes, and what is that like for you?"

"It's amazing!" she says. "And unusual! I want to try this more. It feels so peaceful."

"Joanie, how do you feel connected to this environment?"

She takes a moment to look out over the field before answering, then nods slowly, smiles, and says, "I feel like, just as the leaves are changing, so am I. That actually feels really secure to me, and reassuring." I notice that her speech has slowed down as she adds, "I think I need to accept some of the changes in my own life."

COGNITIVE BEHAVIORAL THERAPY

Like many therapists, I consider cognitive behavioral therapy (CBT) a backbone of my practice. This therapeutic intervention is all about the overlap of thoughts, feelings, and behaviors, with a key focus on recognizing the ones that feel automatic and learning to reframe them into something more productive. CBT training includes the use of manuals and treatment protocols. A well-trained and experienced CBT therapist will be able to learn about their client and then fluidly integrate CBT principles into their individual cases. I find that CBT theories and principles show up in every session. Clients seem to appreciate the information that CBT teaches them, as well as the neutral tone it offers for making their issues feel understandable and approachable.

CBT therapists often utilize worksheets to help clients implement strategies. Since it would be a bit cumbersome to walk around with a backpack full of papers, I keep CBT worksheets in a folder in the photos section of my phone, so I can easily share and discuss them on the go. However, walking therapy can often serve as a "living worksheet" for clients. With a little practice, therapists can use their surroundings to work creatively within their existing framework of therapeutic skills. Here are just a few examples.

CATASTROPHIZING

One easy CBT concept to explain in a walk and talk session is catastrophizing, an automatic thought process in which your brain takes an event you are concerned about and blows it out of proportion to the point of becoming fearful. Say a client starts our session talking about their fear of taking a standardized test. If they do poorly, they might say, they won't get into their choice college, which would mean becoming a total failure, probably having no job, and eventually dying on the streets.

To help them see the absurdity of this progression, I might say to them, "I'm kind of scared of going down that path we are heading toward because there may be a bear hiding in the trees. If we keep going, we might get attacked, probably get eaten, and die right here on the trail." In most cases, my client typically gets the parallel and realizes how catastrophizing stops us from reaching our goals before we even have a chance to assess whether our fears are reasonable.

OBSESSIVE-COMPULSIVE DISORDER

My colleague Julie Edwards, a social worker in Pembroke, Ontario, recently did a walk and talk session with a woman who struggles with OCD and has been working on her ability to let some things go. After identifying the client's urge to remove sticks from the trail along the way, Julie guided her client to practice resisting that urge. This form of CBT-based exposure therapy served as a powerful metaphor for how she can better manage her OCD and stress in general. The client's success in leaving some sticks untouched inspired her to release control in certain aspects of her life.

DIALECTICAL BEHAVIORAL THERAPY

Tammie Rosenbloom, a clinical social worker in Minneapolis, found a way to utilize dialectical behavior therapy (DBT, an offshoot of CBT) with a twenty-four-year-old male client as they walked a paved path around a lake. After walking for twenty minutes, they found a park bench off the path where they could sit comfortably and privately. Using the workbook she'd brought in her backpack, Tammie taught the client core mindfulness skills, then used their surroundings to help him practice those skills: smelling the air, listening to the interplay of nature sounds and city noises, observing the way their bodies were positioned on the bench, touching grass and stones beside them. Afterward, they practiced mindful walking until they were back at their starting point.

TRAUMA-INFORMED THERAPY

Given that trauma victims frequently feel unsafe in their bodies, walking therapy lends itself particularly well to a trauma-informed approach. As Dr. Bessel van der Kolk (2014) writes in *The Body Keeps the Score*, "People who cannot comfortably notice what is going on inside become vulnerable to respond to any sensory shift, either by shutting down or going into a panic" (p. 99) and "in order to change, people need to become aware of their sensations and the way that their bodies interact with the world around them. Physical self-awareness is the first step in releasing the tyranny of the past" (p. 103).

When used as a stand-alone technique, or when combined with other trauma-informed techniques (such as EMDR, somatic experiencing, or mindfulness-based stress reduction), walking is a grounding practice that can provide clients with a healthy sense of agency through reconnecting positively with their bodies.

Since being knowledgeable about trauma is imperative for therapists these days, here is an example of how I've integrated the techniques of trauma-informed therapy into my walk and talk sessions.

• • • • •

Taylor, a twenty-one-year-old White woman, is a starting defender on her college soccer team who began seeing me for therapy a year ago when she started having panic attacks before games. She has worked with focus and intention on managing her stress and understanding the science behind her anxiety. Within a few months, she was able to identify when she felt the anxiety rising, catch it before it escalated, and engage her parasympathetic nervous system to bring the pressure down—in her words, "kill the panic before it kills me." As an athlete, she learned quickly how to work through the stress-response cycle by doing short exercises (mantras, positive self-talk, self-compassion) to regain her equilibrium prior to games. Thanks to her progress and commitment, we had slowed our sessions down during her second semester, just maintaining monthly check-ins. Then, only a week before beginning her senior year, she called to schedule an appointment. Her voice shaking, Taylor told me that she had gone on a date that ended with the man sexually assaulting her. Later that week, we meet up at our usual trail.

Deep in the forest, with light shining down from cracks in the tree canopy, Taylor leads the way up the rugged path, raising dust with each forceful step she takes. I trek behind, letting her set the pace as she replays the scene in which the man did not respect her boundaries. She describes how it felt to have lost control, and she cries, remembering how alone and afraid she felt that night and the feeling of shame and humiliation that she was left with. Between tears of confusion and anger, she says to me, "I just froze. I couldn't do anything. What's wrong with me?"

For some clients, I might simply hold space in this moment. For Taylor, I've learned, it helps to understand the science behind the thoughts and behaviors she struggles with. Offering a tissue, I gently tell her, "Taylor, your freeze response was completely normal, especially in an assault situation. Your nervous system was trying very hard to keep you as safe as possible. It was your body saying that you needed to shut down in order to survive. Freezing is not a weakness; it is your smart mind and body's way of taking care of itself."

As we climb the hill and Taylor shares more about her experience that night, her anger becomes increasingly obvious in her voice, her words, and her body. The hike up the hill has become a way to let out her rage. Not only does the physical exertion help Taylor acknowledge her feelings by channeling them into something "productive," but it also helps focus her awareness on her own strength, bringing back the sense that she *does* have control over her own body. She begins to talk about healing and wanting to feel stronger. She vows never to come into contact with the man again and to maintain a sense of strength and dignity despite the position he'd put her in.

By this time, we've reached the top of the hill. I ask her to take a breath, drink some water, and notice her achievement. As we glance down at the steep climb we've just accomplished, Taylor declares through a mess of tears, "I did that!"

For my part, I am sweating through my shirt, my legs are trembling, and I am ready for an extra gallon of water. But I put these concerns aside to ask Taylor, "How are you feeling?"

I expect her to answer that she's exhausted or spent. Instead, she surprises me by saying how good she feels—the climb, the heat, and the sweat have been so cathartic. Taylor's rigorous training regimen has accustomed her to "sweating through" challenges; in fact, her usual coping skills include running, weightlifting, and, of course, practicing soccer. Talking while exerting herself physically feels natural and very comfortable to her.

As we make our way back down the trail, we talk about her support system. Taylor lists a few friends whom she can call on anytime—in fact, she already has plans to go swimming with her friend the next day. Reflecting on how meaningful those friendships are to her and how positive physical activities keep her focused on the good things in life, Taylor reminds herself out loud, "Crappy things, like what happened to me the other night, will not break me. I am stronger than that, and I have so many good things to look forward to. I am strong and resilient."

PLAY THERAPY

Play is how children learn about themselves. It's also how they communicate ideas and experiences that are beyond their emotional or mental vocabulary. Outdoor play therapy invites the child to play out their stories using natural objects, encouraging creativity and resulting in insights that don't always occur in an office environment, even with the usual toolbox of dolls and figurines. As you'll see from the following examples, there are numerous ways to incorporate outdoor play therapy during walk and talk sessions throughout the year.

WINTER

- Playing in snow, making snow angels, building sculptures out of snow
- Trying to catch a snowflake on your tongue
- Throwing snowballs
- Breathing out to create frost
- Sledding

SPRING

- Climbing on rocks
- Playing on a playground
- Jumping in puddles
- Picking or smelling flowers

SUMMER

- Drawing insects, butterflies, birds, or flowers
- Wading in a creek
- Skipping stones
- Hiking around and through water
- Crossing streams on fallen logs

FALL

- Collecting acorns
- Crunching leaves underfoot
- Jumping into piles of leaves
- Collecting colorful leaves and pressing them in a book
- Looking for animals like worms, bugs, and toads under rocks
- Noticing the trees sway in the breeze
- Watching the clouds float by

Jumping in puddles or throwing snowballs can be a way to release heavy emotions or compulsions like perfectionism, while crunching leaves underfoot can allow children to release feelings of anger, shame, or rejection. Looking for creatures under rocks is a great way to illustrate uncovering layers within ourselves to reveal something fantastic beneath.

Each of these play-based activities helps bring meaning and feeling into your clients' stories, supporting the emotions that they are trying to express or understand for themselves. Connecting to the natural world can encourage your clients to understand that they are an integral part of a bigger world. And as I've discovered, these techniques aren't limited to young children—I've incorporated outdoor play into walk and talk sessions with teens and even adults. The following story offers a great example of how creative use of play therapy can enhance the walk and talk experience.

• • • • •

Shantay, a thirteen-year-old Black girl, was adopted at just two weeks old by an interracial couple—her mother is Indian and her father is Black. When I first spoke with Mom on the phone, she said, "Her name is spelled S-H-A-N-T-A-Y, which is the name that her birth mom gave her. We decided to honor her birth mom and keep the name. However, we pronounce her name like 'Shanti,' which in Sanskrit means peace." Right away, I discerned that this middle schooler was living in the midst of many different cultures and transitions.

Shantay attends a predominately White school, and within the first week of starting seventh grade, she became the victim of bullying. While she was changing for gym in the locker room, a few girls took her clothes and threw them in the trash; her peers stood by and laughed while she frantically searched for her missing clothes. Since then, her parents said Shantay has acted sad and withdrawn. Along with barely eating and sleeping fitfully, she often stays in bed so late that she misses the first part of school; during lunch, she retreats outside to wander the school grounds alone. Noticing this, a school counselor recommended my practice to Shantay's parents, though they didn't make the call until the day they noticed that Shantay had intentionally cut her arm.

Shantay began meeting with me only four weeks after the bullying incident. At first, she could barely open up about her thoughts and feelings, but after a session or two of building rapport on the trail, she began to trust me. During our third walk and talk session, I ask her if we can talk about the day the girls took her clothes.

Shantay answers, "I don't like to think about it. I feel so bad." Hesitating, she adds, "I mean, I'm just really embarrassed. I had been joking around with the girls and we were kind of teasing each other about changing for gym, how awkward it can be. I am so mad at myself for participating in that in the first place. I should have just changed in my own space and not even talked with them."

Starting to cry, Shantay clenches her fists together as she begins walking faster. Increasing my pace to keep up, I ask her to name some of the feelings she is having in that moment.

"I'm angry," she pants. "Upset with myself. Ashamed."

"Can you find something along the path that could represent those bad feelings?"

Stopping, Shantay picks up a jagged little rock and calls it the "angry rock." Picking up another, she calls it "the ashamed rock." Continuing until both her hands are full of rocks, she looks at me, wondering what to do next.

"Let's pick a place somewhere in the woods to put those rocks down," I suggest.

Finding a little patch of moss at the base of a large tree, Shantay places the pile of rocks on it, then instinctively kicks a pile of brown leaves over it, burying the rocks completely. Turning her back on the pile, she walks back toward me, releasing a big sigh: *"Hhhhhuuuhhh."*

Watching her, I comment, "Wow—I noticed a bit of a relief there." She responds with just a silent nodding of her head, but her steps along the path seem a little less burdened than before.

After a few moments of quietness, I ask another question.

"Shantay, can you please tell me about some good memories you have with friends?"

She responds easily with stories of swimming, hiking, and playing catch with her Girl Scout troop. The memories draw a smile out of her. I ask her to find something on the path that represents these happy feelings. "The red and yellow leaves," she answers and, without being asked, begins to collect some of the brightly colored leaves that lie around us on the path.

I ask her what she wants to do with the leaves.

"I want to bring them home and press them with waxed paper," she says. "I'm going to use the dictionary my dad got me last year to hold them in place."

I respond with a simple reflection, "Hold those good feelings in place."

· · · · ·

Your therapeutic practice is so much more than simply the sum of the techniques or tools you've collected. What ultimately makes your practice effective is what you carry around with you everywhere you go: the practical knowledge you've gained, the insight and skills you've acquired, the unique self you bring to the session. Adapting your office practice to an outdoor setting is just a matter of thinking outside the box. Trust yourself, connect with your environment, and adapt your skills and practices in the way that feels right. Remember, just because it's always been done a certain way doesn't mean that's the only way.

Chapter 4

Therapy in the Time of the COVID-19 Pandemic

When I glance back at my email inbox, I see a stark difference between emails BC (before COVID) and those that came in during the pandemic.

Before: "My teenage daughter seems to be struggling with anxiety. Are you available to see her?"

After: "I really need to get my daughter in to see you. She is refusing teletherapy. She is just not comfortable talking with a stranger over the computer."

This urgency isn't surprising. The COVID-19 pandemic has brought significant anxiety, suffering, and loss to many people's lives. Along with the ever-present threat to our physical health, the pandemic triggered widespread financial hardship, food insecurity, and a host of other social ills, all exacerbated by indefinite gaps in social services that many people relied on for safety and support (everything from the closing of public schools to the devastating effects of shuttered substance abuse treatment programs). Combine that with mandated social isolation, and it's no surprise that we saw a corresponding decline in mental health, particularly within the world's most vulnerable populations. Unfortunately, mental health services were also greatly impacted during this time. According to *The Lancet*, "Reasons for disruption included an insufficient number or redeployment of health workers to the COVID-19 response (in 30% of countries), use of mental health facilities as COVID-19 quarantine or treatment facilities (in 19% of countries), and insufficient supply of personal protective equipment (in 28% of countries)" (The Lancet Infectious Diseases, 2020, p. 1217).

Even as we (hopefully) approach the end of the pandemic's most serious phase, we have entered a new era where telehealth is becoming the norm; in 2020, about three-quarters of the American Psychological Association's member clinicians had reportedly switched to solely teletherapy services (Chiu, 2020). It's a strange shift to navigate, given that our life's work as therapists is all about connection. In the switch to telehealth platforms, our clients lost more than just the physical comfort of a chair—they lost the reliable safe space where they could open up and let go. Now they were hiding out in basements, bathrooms, closets, and cars just to get time with a therapist in private. (For some, the lack of a safe home environment meant they had to stop therapy altogether.) And it certainly didn't help the "therapeutic frame" to have so many therapists challenged by the transition to technology. For so many reasons, FaceTime, Zoom, Doxy, and Simple Practice just aren't the same as an in-person encounter.

Meanwhile, throughout the COVID-19 pandemic, many people had begun looking outdoors to keep their spirits up. We watched skies and seasons changing from one day to the next, looking for nature's guidance through the changes we were undergoing. We watched sunrises and sunsets for reassurance that while much of the world came to a halt, life at the most fundamental level still continued. Eventually, in the face of draining and difficult telehealth sessions, people began to connect the dots and a trend emerged: moving therapy sessions outdoors (Fraga, 2020).

I definitely noticed an increased interest in my practice as the pandemic spread across the country, not only from new clients but also from colleagues calling me for advice on how to move their practices outdoors. Even those who were familiar with walking therapy found that it wasn't as easy as it used to be. Denice Crowe Clark, a walk and talk therapist in Atlanta, shared with me that the pandemic created an issue she'd never confronted in her walk and talk practice: "Because so many of us city dwellers were cooped up in our condos and apartments, and so many of us were seeking freedom and safety outside, everyone converged upon the park, even during work hours," she told me. "It was too crowded and too noisy, and impossible to maintain the proper social distance. I ended up keeping my sessions online far longer than I would have liked. While other therapists were contacting me to learn more about walk and talk so they could return to in-person sessions as soon as possible, I was faced with the opposite problem" (personal communication, May 10, 2022).

Over the months since COVID-19 became part of our reality, I've thought a lot about why clients (and therapists) crave an in-person session so deeply. My conclusion is that it's because people want to experience each other as whole persons. As a therapist, I want to see my client's body language and facial expressions and feel the way their energy communicates their feelings even when they say nothing. I want to walk alongside them so that they feel that they have company in their journey. I want them to experience the comfort of having someone be present for them, and only them, during our time together. And I believe clients want the same things! Real human presence, offered with commitment and compassion, is the most direct and powerful way to make a client feel protected, private, and confident enough within our session to explore the issues that brought them there.

Having discovered for myself that walking therapy provides all these benefits in a unique way, I was happy to consult with therapists who were interested in moving sessions outdoors. I encouraged them to take this new process one step at a time. I reassured them not to worry about everything being perfect. I promised that they would find ways to make this practice their own as they went along.

This wasn't empty encouragement. The more I practice walk and talk therapy, the more I learn about my practice and about the individual I'm there to serve. Just the other day, I was walking with a client who stopped every ten minutes to notice a plant or admire a bird. Her curiosity provided me with special insight into her personality: She was carefree, open-minded, and appreciative of the small things in life, and she loved to explore—all important insights that will certainly contribute to the work we do together. Would I have seen this side of her in an office? Possibly, but walking in nature made these traits apparent in an immediate and visceral way.

This is yet another virtue of walking therapy—you can't always predict where it will lead or what it will offer you. As I've been writing this book, there have been many times when trying to convey the power and meaning in this practice has left me at a loss for words. When that happens, I often go out for a walk myself. With only the peace of the morning surrounding me, my intentions for this book naturally begin to focus. As I climb the hills of my neighborhood, I think about the past ten years of walking therapy and how the efforts, obstacles, and lessons have all propelled me upward on the climb toward better patient care. As so many therapists have discovered in the past few years, there's a special magic in movement that, if we'll only surrender to it, helps us find the path we're meant to be on.

CLOSENESS AND CONNECTION

As post-pandemic problems continue to unfold—lagging social skills, children falling behind academically, anxiety around being in groups—walking therapy continues to be useful for addressing these social anxiety–related issues. After all, being in the presence of a therapist is one way to experience real-life interactions once again. Therapists have been caught in their own case of adjustment disorder, figuring out how to strike a balance between the extreme changes of early 2020 and the new normal of hybrid therapy sessions. It isn't easy, but we adjust again and again in the name of serving our clients.

A young client recently asked me, as we walked along the nature trail, "Why do the tree branches grow over the path? And why do the tree branches on the other side of the path also arch over the road?"

I answered, "Because we are all looking for connection. We need each other. The trees need to share each other's oxygen and nutrients in order to grow. We were never meant to be alone. Our connection to one another is what helps us grow and be sustained."

As things continue to change and evolve, this is what I keep in mind. No matter what further changes come our way, the ultimate goal of our work is to build closeness and connection with the client that supports them in their journey. Finding our way through this changing world can be hard, but as I've discovered, we can get through just about anything as long as we can be together.

Winter:

Revealing the Roots of
Walk and Talk Therapy

> " You can't stay in your corner of the forest waiting for others to come to you. You have to go to them sometimes. "

—A. A. Milne

Chapter 5

What Does the Research Tell Us About Walk and Talk Therapy?

One morning, while doing my daily internet scour for walk and talk news, I came across an exciting new article titled "Into the Wild: A Meta-Synthesis of Talking Therapy in Natural Outdoor Spaces" (Cooley et al., 2020). Since I was about to meet some colleagues for coffee, I printed the article to read while I waited for them to arrive. Luckily for me, the first colleague who showed up was eager to listen! The article presented loads of academic research confirming the benefits of outdoor, movement-based therapy—benefits I had been trying to formulate in my mind over years of practicing walk and talk—such as:

- Natural spaces have been found to support clients who may not otherwise engage with therapy (Scheinfeld et al., 2011).

- Clients benefit not only from the talking therapy, but also from the restorative effects of nature (Berger, 2009).

- Clients and practitioners feel a greater sense of shared ownership of a natural space (Berger & McLeod, 2006).

- An office setting or a more formal face-to-face encounter can be anxiety provoking for some clients (Jordan & Marshall, 2010).

- For some practitioners, practicing therapy outdoors cultivates a more authentic or human-centered approach that can get lost in clinical settings (Santostefano, 2008).

By now, you've caught on that walking therapy is the great love of my professional life. I get really excited when I see walking therapy receiving more attention, not only from the clinical community but also from academia. After practicing this form of therapy for so many years, it's a great feeling to see walk and talk get its due, especially with a cherry on top like the one that concluded the article: "Recent studies of counsellors, clinical psychologists, and psychotherapists highlight positive experiences of taking therapy outdoors. Their anecdotal accounts and qualitative evidence suggest mental health outcomes are at least as effective, if not more effective in certain individuals, than those obtained indoors" (Cooley et al., 2020, p. 2).

Needless to say, I couldn't agree more!

A HEALTHY MIND IN A HEALTHY BODY

Validation isn't the only reason I get excited about this article and others like it. I also love learning more of the science that makes this practice so uniquely effective. So for this chapter, let's dig into some of the biological considerations for walk and talk.

There is a Latin saying you may have heard: *Mens sana in corpore sano*. It means "a healthy mind in a healthy body." Well-known in medical and fitness circles, this phrase comes from a second-century Roman poem that lists what is most desirable in life; the whole line reads, "You should pray for a healthy mind in a healthy body." As you see, the idea of a mind-body connection has been around a long time. It's only recently in human history that we started treating them as separate.

For millions of years, humans lived with body and mind well integrated. Stress wasn't a mental health issue—it involved real threats to our survival, like wild beasts or natural disasters. The autonomic nervous system (ANS) was our greatest defense, keeping us in a state of fight-or-flight so we could make the quick decisions that would let us live another day.

Time went on, and we moved from a hunting-gathering society to a city-state civilization. We separated ourselves from nature through stone houses, fortresses, and walled cities. While we no longer faced the same degree of environmental threat that our ancestors did, we became our own enemies in some ways, trading the stress of saber-toothed tiger attacks and continent-dividing earthquakes for the stress of poverty, oppression, disease, and war. (Soon to be followed by close-call car accidents, standardized tests, and running late for everything.)

Nevertheless, after all these years, our ANS remains the same as it always was. It greets every instance of stress with a racing heart, a breakout of cold sweat, and a red-alert message running on repeat in our minds: *Do something!* Most of the time, however, there is no oncoming animal to spear, no cave in which to run and hide. So we tell ourselves (or force ourselves) to chill out one way or another. Maybe we give ourselves a rousing pep talk in the mirror. Maybe we duck out early for happy hour. Maybe we ride the elliptical trainer until we can't think anymore. Maybe we keep it all inside, only to unload on a friend or loved one later.

Our keyed-up bodies are hopelessly out of sync with our overloaded minds. Looking at them as two separate parts only makes the situation worse. This may be because we expect the logical part of our brains (left) to function under duress, when in actuality it's the emotional part (right) that wants to take over in those situations. Walk and talk reunites the two sides with its unique combination of movement, nature, and therapy. We touched on this magic elixir briefly in chapter 3, but let's get in there and really examine what's happening in our brains and bodies when we bring them back together.

WALKING HELPS US COMPLETE THE STRESS-RESPONSE CYCLE

While nobody enjoys stress, a well-balanced ANS allows us to manage stress and its accompanying emotions without too much disruption to our everyday functioning. However, when the ANS gets out of balance, our sympathetic nervous system is chronically activated, causing (among other things) our breathing to shorten, our heart rate to increase, and sometimes even panic attacks or other major stress reactions. The more out of balance the ANS becomes, the more vulnerable we are to other types of illness.

As science continues to reveal, what happens upstairs is mimicked closely by what happens downstairs. Thanks to the gut-brain axis, a biochemical signaling system between the gastrointestinal tract and the central nervous system, the serotonin that floods our brains in "feel good" moments will send the same signals all the way to our bellies. In the same way, the growling of an empty stomach will be closely followed by grouchy or unpleasant thoughts until we finally eat a snack—we literally have hunger on the brain!

Given the close connection between mental health and physical health, heart rate variability (HRV) is a commonly used method for measuring how our bodies are handling the impact of mental and emotional stress. A higher HRV indicates a healthier, more resilient system. This is why doctors will recommend activities like distance running or yoga to people who are suffering from the effects of chronic stress—both of these activities improve your HRV by developing internal and external balance. (You know what else improves HRV? I'll give you one guess . . .)

Still, resilience doesn't mean "stress free." Even with a high HRV and other healthy habits, we can get hit at times with burdens that feel too heavy to carry. This is where we part ways with the rest of the animal kingdom. In *Why Zebras Don't Get Ulcers*, neuroendocrinology researcher Robert M. Sapolsky (2004) discusses how a human's response to stress takes longer to move through the body than an animal's response. Simply put, our stressors are not as easy to "outrun." While a gazelle can look behind them and see that a lion is no longer chasing them, humans rarely receive an analogous moment regarding threats like financial insecurity, relationship anxiety, systemic injustice, or chronic illness. The physical toll of all this unresolved stress only adds to our mental burden, creating a constant flow of stress hormones between the brain and the gut that builds over time until something finally crashes and burns.

So how do we turn this negative cycle in the right direction? In the book *Burnout: The Secret to Unlocking the Stress Cycle*, authors Emily and Amelia Nagoski (2019) show that a stressful situation (e.g., public speaking, a looming deadline, concern for a loved one) isn't really the problem—it's how we deal with it that makes the difference. They write, "The strategies that deal with stressors have almost no relationship to the strategies that deal with the physiological reactions our bodies have to those stressors. To be 'well' is not to live in a state of perpetual safety and calm, but to move fluidly from a state of adversity, risk, adventure, or excitement, back to safety and calm, and out again" (p. 27). Unsurprisingly, their recommendations for completing the stress cycle start with physical activity. According to their research, physical movement helps move stress through our system, allowing us to release the stress, complete the cycle, and avoid the crash. Along with movement, the *Burnout* authors recommend things such as breathwork, positive social interaction, release of emotions (laughing or crying), and creative expression (singing, painting, storytelling, etc.).

Anyone else notice that these are all things we do within the walking therapy session? Some of it may require encouragement or guidance from the therapist, but often, these other beneficial activities just happen organically during the walking therapy session. The following story offers a great example.

• • • • •

Taylor and I arrive at our parking lot at the exact same time. The ground is blanketed in a fine layer of snow, the sky is gray, and there are delicate icicles on the branches of the trees. Taylor hops out of her car wearing a college sweatshirt, a puffy black vest, and a bright pink fuzzy hat—she is dressed to deal with the cold. I greet her and we start toward the trail.

"I literally just finished my exams last night, and I am so exhausted," Taylor tells me. "The finals were so freaking hard, and I have no idea if I passed, but I'm just glad to be done at this point."

I respond, "Congratulations on finishing the semester. Sounds like you had a pretty heavy course load. What an accomplishment!"

"Yeah. It feels really good to be done. Not gonna lie, it was a struggle." She laughs nervously and looks concerned.

"I see that you are relieved to be done but also worried about the outcome of the semester," I observe. "Is anything else going on for you?"

"Well, I haven't had a chance to really hang out with my friends much, because of all the studying. And I'm looking forward to seeing my high school friends who are coming home for break." She pauses. "And, well, uh, I'm actually pretty upset because I happened to see a Facebook post from . . . you know, the guy. It just reminded me of him and that night, and . . . oh, I don't know. It just felt crappy."

She begins to walk faster, heading straight for our favorite hill. This time, I'm prepared to take it on. I know how therapeutic this route is for Taylor—this hill seems to help her solve her problems in a way nothing else does.

As we trudge onward, Taylor opens up some more. "I wish I could just block him out of my mind. You know, just forget that it ever happened. But being reminded of him because something online jumped out in front of me. I feel so powerless. So out of control."

"Taylor, I'm so sorry that you're going through this," I say. "I want you to notice the difference between then and now. Can you check in with your body and notice what it's doing now?"

"Yeah." She pauses. "It's like, I'm thinking worried and angry thoughts, but my body is saying a different thing. I'm feeling really good in my body. I mean, a little tired, but strong and tough." She offers a quick, rosy-cheeked smile before we attack the hill. I hear her breathing heavily as we climb—there's intention in that breath, a focus on the healing nature of her inhales and exhales. Her movements are strong and her strides are long. After a few minutes, we reach the top of the hill and observe the surroundings.

"Wow," says Taylor. "It's so beautiful up here—look at this view. And the snow is just so pretty. I love the icicles and the way the trees are a little droopy."

Just then, I have an idea. "Taylor, do you want to try something goofy?"

Used to my antics by now, she laughs, "Sure!"

"What if we take a stick and write 'What's His Name' in the snow, and then stamp it out?"

"Yes! Please!" Taylor finds a space in the ground that has a flat place to etch in the snow. Folding herself over toward the ground, she begins to write the name; it's not long before she starts to cry, and I stand by to hold and witness the pain she is experiencing. After a minute, though, she exerts an audible exhale, followed by a huge inhale, then flings the stick through the air over the side of the hill.

Looking at me, she says, "Ready? Will you stomp with me?"

I nod in agreement, and the two of us go to town. As we stomp out the letters, Taylor begins to holler: "Goodbye. See ya. Adios. I don't need this memory. You no longer rule me." We look down and no longer see the writing; instead, we see lots of hard-earned footprints.

"That felt so amazing!" Taylor takes another deep breath. "I feel like I really made my own decision there. That I don't need to let him or the memory of him control me."

As we make our way back through the snow-covered forest, we talk about how Taylor can adapt this as needed, from writing on paper and crumpling it up or burning it to other creative methods, like writing on a fogged window and then wiping it clean. When we get back to our cars, she says again, "I feel so much better."

I say to her, "You really moved from pain to a much better place for yourself. Think about all the things you did to move through the stress-response cycle. You cried, you laughed, you talked, you moved, you created (and destroyed), and you breathed!"

We give each other a high five and share a genuine laugh.

WALKING CREATES CONNECTION WITH BREATH

If you've ever tried to do some calming breathwork in the midst of a busy day—or, for that matter, attempted to "cure" a panic attack with a few deep breaths—you know that connecting with your breath can be a lot harder in practice than in theory. Compare that to how easily breath connection comes when you're hiking a mountain, practicing yoga, or just taking a walk around the block for some fresh air.

As Bessel van der Kolk (2014) writes in *The Body Keeps the Score*, "Scientific methods have confirmed that changing the way one breathes can improve problems with anger, depression, and anxiety" (pp. 270–271). Specifically, deep inhalations and long exhalations inherently engage the parasympathetic nervous system, regulating stress and stabilizing mood. While I'm all for breathwork on its own, exercises like walking naturally trigger our bodies to engage in deep, slow, regulated breathing. In other words, walking can make a body-breath connection instantly accessible for people who struggle to master a breathwork technique or to make time for it in their busy schedule.

WALKING "CURES" STAGNANT THOUGHTS AND BEHAVIORS

Think for a moment about your own patterns with energy, focus, and attention. How do you focus best? While we tend to associate the word *focus* with someone hunched over a desk peering intently at what's in front of them, most of us have had the experience of looking up from the book we're studying or the screen we're working on and realizing we haven't been mentally "there" for quite some time. What do we do in these situations? We move around! Get up from the desk, give our body a shake, step outside for some fresh air, and maybe . . . take a walk?

A number of prominent studies have looked at how physical movement can assist with extended focus and concentration. A study published in *Frontiers in Psychology* (Rassovsky & Alfassi, 2019) not only confirmed the brain benefits of regular exercise for the increasingly sedentary adult lifestyle, but also indicated that incorporating physical activity into "attentional" tasks can bolster cognitive performance. The authors had an even bolder recommendation: "These findings could be readily translated to practical applications in the classroom or working environment. Pedaling on a stationary bicycle or walking on a treadmill during lecture or work may prove beneficial for both physical and brain health" (p. 4).

I've seen remarkable proof of this benefit during sessions with patients who have an ADHD diagnosis. There's an undeniable "buzz" about these folks, which immediately manifests in how fast they walk (and talk). The current diagnostic checklist for ADHD includes "often on the go" and acting as if "driven by a motor"—such a great description for the patients I've seen with hyperactivity. Interestingly, when we start the session walking at a pace that meets their energy level, the client often slows down eventually and is able to focus more deeply and intentionally on their inner work. It's worth noting that these clients are some of the biggest fans of walk and talk I've ever met! They often express what a relief it is to be outdoors rather than inside an office, and how much better it feels to be moving while they talk.

Tammie Rosenbloom, a walk and talk therapist in Minneapolis, tells of a similarly powerful moment with a teenage boy who was in recovery from substance use disorder. She said that the teen had complained of being bored, and his urges to relapse were often fueled by a lack of fun activities and sober friends. When Tammie suggested they try something different by meeting at the city lake to walk, the client was visibly excited to be outdoors instead of in the office. While walking, they saw fish jumping in the lake. The client proceeded to tell Tammie about his love of fishing. Thinking back to the summers he'd spent at his grandmother's cabin in the woods, he educated Tammie about everything from the types of fish he enjoyed catching to the specific lures used. By the end of their walk, he was talking about resuming his fishing hobby and even teaching kids how to fish. The decision to move the session outdoors seemed to give the client a hard reset, offering him a fresh vision of the kind of life he wanted to lead.

At this point, I can't even imagine sitting in a session anymore with a person whose energy or emotions are ready to explode. Walking is a too-good-to-miss opportunity for them to learn how they can use physical movement to face their thoughts and feelings and find meaning in their current situation.

As you'll see in the following story, while Jake, the client who had recently lost his wife, had plenty of experience using exercise to relieve his feelings, our walk and talk sessions showed him how movement could actually transform his thoughts over time.

· · · · ·

I get to our meeting place early and sit snugly in my car's eighty-degree heat until Jake arrives. When I see his car pull up, I bundle myself in all my layers, brace myself to face the crisp, cold air, and step out of my car with a warm smile. (Even smiles can help warm things up!) However, as we venture out for our walk, a sullen mood sets in.

"I'm thinking about the last Christmas I had with her," Jake blurts out. "It was almost like old times—she was in great spirits, she had more energy than she'd had in a while. I could almost believe that everything was going to get better. But deep down, I knew it would be our last holiday together."

The frigid air whips around us as the sun desperately tries to compensate. Mirroring the weather, a lot of coldness surrounds Jake's memories of that time. Over the past six sessions, I have been working with Jake on reaching emotions that surround his grief and loss. Today, the rhythm of our footsteps is a background percussion for the feelings that he starts to acknowledge, each word accompanied by his heavy footfall:

"Sadness." *Thump.*

"Grief." *Thump.*

"Loss." *Thump.*

"Loneliness." *Thump.*

"Pain." *Thump.*

As our pace picks up, I unwrap my scarf and unzip the top of my coat. The cool air on my neck reminds me of a technique I once learned in a trauma training for helping clients not feel isolated in their painful memories.

"The layers of pain run very deep for you," I say to Jake. "Even while you're thinking about her most of the time, you are also functioning. Doing your job, running errands, taking care of the kids. Just like the layers of clothes we put on today to keep ourselves warm, we wear emotional layers to shield ourselves from unbearable pain. But we can also incorporate the positive memories—the meaningful moments—as layers that comfort and protect us as we heal. Tell me about the holidays before she was sick. Tell me what it was like at your house and what you did as a family."

Jake's smile warms as he tells me about those good times: the traditions, the everyday routines, the moments that felt full of joy and promise. He talks about the warmth of the kitchen, the sweet smells of home-baked bread, the upbeat carols playing on the radio. As the percussion of his footsteps is joined by the music of his memories, Jake seems to walk a bit more upright. He releases his hands from his pockets, his arms swinging as he explores this new territory of emotion.

As we near the end of our walk, he tells me that he plans to call some friends and invite them over for Christmas. He wants to give his kids a meaningful day to celebrate and maintain a strong connection with his support system. After receiving so much during this hard time, he's ready to give again.

• • • • •

Now that we've dug deep into how walking helps the body and mind reconnect, let's look at the effect of spending time outdoors.

HOW THE OUTDOORS IMPACTS MENTAL HEALTH

The word *biophilia* first appeared in psychoanalyst Erich Fromm's 1973 book *The Anatomy of Human Destructiveness*. In contrast to the concept of necrophilia (interest in death and destruction), Fromm described biophilia as "the passionate love of life and of all that is alive; it is the wish to further growth, whether in a person, a plant, an idea, or a social group" (p. 406). Just over a decade later, the prolific biologist Edward O. Wilson chose this word as the title of his 1984 memoir. Reflecting on his decades of natural research, *Biophilia: The Human Bond with Other Species* lays out a hypothesis that feels both groundbreaking and obvious at the same time: Being alive means having a natural connection with all living things.

"Biophilia," Wilson writes, "is the innately emotional affiliation of human beings to other living organisms. Innate means hereditary and hence part of ultimate human nature" (1993, p. 31). At the same time, he acknowledges that this affinity can be shaped and limited by our experiences and influences. "Biophilia, like other patterns of complex behavior, is likely to be mediated by rules of prepared and counter prepared learning—the tendency to learn or to resist learning certain responses as opposed to others. . . . The feelings molded by the learning rules fall along several emotional spectra: from attraction to aversion, from awe to indifference, from peacefulness to fear-driven anxiety" (p. 31).

Wilson's hypothesis suggests that regardless of how you consciously feel about being in nature, your primitive brain responds to it like a prodigal child returning home. Studies show that just the sight of natural bodies of water or unboundaried green space provides an instant calming effect to the nervous system. Add in other sensory stimuli like the warm living earth under your feet, or the scent of pine and cedar in the air, and the effects become even more pronounced: a refreshed mood, increased self-esteem, and decreased feelings of isolation. As Martin Jordan (2014) writes in *Nature and Therapy*, "The Biophilia Hypothesis is often used to support the idea of an evolutionary relationship with nature that is not purely biological but is linked to psychology and identity" (p. 9).

Of course, none of this is news to people from indigenous cultures, many of which are defined and sustained by their connection to nature. Indigenous peoples from the U.S. to Australia have held a worldview that regards all living things—humans, animals, and plants—as equals, and thus related at an existential, even spiritual, level. This belief not only endows them with a sense of responsibility to care for the earth, but also offers a powerful sense of well-being in nature.

In the 1980s, Japan established the custom of *shinrin-yoku* or "forest bathing." This practice of short, leisurely visits to a forest has demonstrated that exposure to nature creates calming neuropsychological effects through changes in the nervous system. In 2004, Yoshifumi Miyazaki and Juyoung Lee published their findings that "leisurely forest walks, compared to urban walks, deliver a 12 percent decrease in cortisol levels, . . . a 7 percent decrease in sympathetic nerve activity, a 1.4 percent decrease in blood pressure, and a 6 percent decrease in heart rate" (Williams, 2017, p. 23). Participants also reported better moods and lowered anxiety.

The medical establishment is just beginning to catch up to this ancestral wisdom, as more and more studies confirm the healing powers of being outdoors:

- A 2012 study found that thinking about a painful memory while spending time in nature is particularly beneficial for people suffering from depression. Moreover, the beneficial effects observed in individuals with a major depressive disorder (MDD) were nearly five times as large as those observed in healthy individuals (Berman et al., 2012).

- A 2019 study saw a 20 to 30 percent decrease in salivary stress biomarkers after subjects spent just 30 minutes exposed to nature (Hunter et al., 2019).

- In a 2022 study, researchers attached a portable EEG device to participants while they were immersed in therapeutic gardens and watched in real time as the subjects' brains showed measurable improvement from depressive disorders (Olszewska-Guizzo et al., 2022).

None of this should be surprising, considering the well-known science behind just a few of the basic elements of a walk in the woods. Being in nature means exposure to sunlight, which in turn triggers the body to produce vitamin D, an essential hormone that our increasingly indoor lifestyles have made harder to come by. The symptoms of vitamin D deficiency—lower energy, eating and sleeping too much, and being less social—look a lot like depression. If you've ever struggled with seasonal affective disorder, you know that just going outside for fifteen minutes or so, even when the day is short and the sunlight is weak, can give you a new lease on life. Imagine what that can do for people struggling with depression!

Research is one thing, but what's really exciting is how western medicine has responded to it. Some doctors have actually begun writing "nature prescriptions" to treat ADHD, anxiety, diabetes, asthma, and other chronic health conditions. Pediatrician Dr. Robert Zarr has taken it one step further by creating the ParkRx America platform (available at https://parkrxamerica.org), where doctors, therapists, and other health care providers can access a step-by-step walk-through to write a nature prescription, save it in the patient's chart, and (if the patient desires) schedule automated reminders for the patient, increasing the likelihood that they will "fill" their prescription. It's not hard to imagine a future in which the first line of treatment for physical and mental health is a "nature pill." No side effects, no risky interactions with foods or other medications, and no cost? Talk about a wonder drug!

THIS IS YOUR BRAIN ON NATURE

It's not only nature's physical inputs that make the impact. In the book *Awestruck*, psychologist Jonah Paquette (2020) writes about the brain's default mode network (DMN), an area of the brain that lights up when you're checked out—daydreaming, self-analyzing, ruminating on the past, worrying about the future—any brain activity that isn't focused on the here and now. There's just one thing that can shut down the DMN: experiencing awe. Awe can come from any environment, activity, or interaction that gets you out of your head and into the world around you in a way that helps you feel safe, connected, and glad to be alive. Experiences of awe in nature have been shown to boost mood, lower levels of inflammatory cytokines, and improve the immune system (Stellar et al., 2015).

I was recently walking with a client who, in her words, couldn't get a break from her thoughts. She talked about being stressed out and tired of hearing herself think. Then, out of nowhere, a huge shadow passed over us, stopping us in our tracks. We looked up to see a blue heron perched on a branch forty feet above us, gazing regally over the swath of swampland. We stood in silent awe of its beauty and serenity; minutes went by before we moved or even looked at each other. My client commented on the creature's elegance, and on the rarity of an extended encounter like this one. When I asked how she was feeling, she responded, "Amazed . . . and relaxed." I'll admit I was a little reluctant to bring us back to our conversation, but when I asked her to describe her thoughts to me at that point, she said, "I did notice that I stopped thinking about my thinking!"

Over the past several years, there has been a widespread renewal in research regarding the effects of nature on our health, with new studies coming out regularly about how spending time outdoors effectively combats the rise of ills such as obesity, anxiety, and depression. Life in the time of COVID was a prime time for putting these studies to the test, as millions of people around the world took to the trails for much-needed time and space to relieve stress and feel their feelings. Still, there's one important piece of the puzzle that these studies haven't addressed, which was illuminated for me by my colleague Jules Taylor Shore, a neurobiology teacher, academic, and therapist who can synthesize everything she's ever read into something that makes sense. When I asked her professional opinion on what makes walking so effective for mental health, Jules came through with her usual profound simplicity: "We are walking people" (personal communication, May 26, 2022).

As Jules explains it, our evolution into upright walking is about more than just efficiency of movement—it also speaks to humankind's other distinguishing factor: our advanced brains. As we discussed in chapter 3, walking integrates the left and right hemispheres of the brain through bilateral movement. The left side of the brain sees the world as a functional tool, getting us from point A to point B safely and efficiently, while the right side is invested in the here and now, keeping us open to surprise and relationship along our journey. When we walk, we stimulate each side equally, integrating both functions together, with the result being that our brains feel simultaneously safe and expansive. When another human being is walking alongside us, that brain state is confirmed—we feel the comfort and affirmation of belonging to our tribe. "When we walk with a shared rhythm," said Jules, "we are undoing aloneness" (personal communication, May 26, 2022).

· · · · ·

Today is a particularly bright winter day. The sun is shining, and the cold air is refreshing. I walk with Joanie on the path that leads toward the pond. She begins by bringing up a concern regarding her social anxiety.

"I am so nervous about this holiday party that I'm supposed to go to next week."

"Yes. Tell me more about it and the feelings you are experiencing."

"First of all, it's for work, and work holiday parties usually suck, right? I mean, people are drinking, and I don't drink. Then they are overly friendly. Also, not everyone knows that I'm gay, so sometimes awkward things happen."

"Sounds like you have some experience with this?"

She responds with a big sigh, "Yeah. Last year these people were making homophobic jokes, and it was super-duper uncomfortable. I just felt so icky and out of place."

I nod and take note that Joanie is walking pretty fast now, heading toward a bench at the edge of the pond. She asks, "Can we just sit for a few minutes?"

"Of course. I know you like this bench and the pond here."

We sit down on the cold wooden bench and look out at the pond. There is ice around the edges, but the middle still ripples with open water, and there are birds nesting in the tall grasses that surround the pond.

Joanie reflects, "I love this spot because it is so calm and peaceful. When there is so much going on in the world around me, I like to just sit in a place where I can watch the water and the birds, and let nature 'happen.' Like, I don't have to pretend to be someone else. I don't have to make so many stressful choices about how to behave. I feel sometimes like I lead two lives. At least here, in nature, I can just be me."

I respond, "So in a way, the natural environment validates who you are." She nods in agreement, and I follow with a question, "Joanie, let me ask about what it might be like for you to be yourself at this party. Can you try to imagine that you are you and don't need to pretend to be someone else?"

She thinks deeply for a minute or two. "Scary thought," she murmurs.

"What's so scary about that?"

"Just worrying about what people think about me. I guess it's a fear of judgment."

I nod. "I was just wondering if there's a flip side to that. What would it be like for you to be you?"

"Kind of badass, in a way," she admits. "Just to go out there and be me—the raw me, not someone others think I need to be."

All of a sudden, we are back on the path, walking again at a rapid pace. Something seems to have activated Joanie and she really needs to get going. We zip through the leafless trees, the brown grass, the raw frozen dirt. Finally, Joanie glances over at me with wide eyes and says, "I want to try it. I will slay!"

"Wow, yes! Go you!"

COMING HOME TO OUR BIOME

There's a word in biology that has been gaining ground in our everyday conversations: *biome*. While the word usually refers to a regional "community" of plants, animals, and other living things, it can also be used to describe social communities, such as our families or circles of close friends.

If you think about it, therapy is another type of biome. No matter where the therapeutic conversation happens, it welcomes clients into shared ownership of space and a restorative connection. It's a context in which we help our clients feel safe enough to be their truest selves, express their honest thoughts, and feel the full power of their deepest, rawest emotions. Connecting the therapeutic biome with time spent outdoors is one of the greatest services we can offer our clients. It shows them that there is an entire world out there waiting to welcome them, just as they are. The more they go to that place for unconditional acceptance, the more they learn to accept themselves.

Chapter 6

The History of Walk and Talk Therapy

What's the first thing that comes to mind when you think of Freud? His couch? His cigar? Dreams? The id, ego, and superego? His seminal (and sometimes controversial) contributions to the field of psychotherapy?

For me, any mention of Freud is an invitation to talk about his contributions to walking therapy. Google it—it's a fascinating rabbit trail to follow. My favorite story involves Freud and the renowned German composer Gustav Mahler. (No worries about breaching client confidentiality—Mahler died over 100 years ago.)

According to the story, back in 1910, Mahler was suffering deeply after discovering that his wife had been having an affair, so he reached out to Freud for psychoanalysis. The story continues that, following a marathon four-hour walking therapy session with Freud, Mahler went on to compose "Symphony No. 10," a work that stands out for its raw emotionality and shocking use of dissonance. Many music scholars speculate that Mahler was working out the turmoil of his life at the time through this music. Clearly, his session with Freud brought some deep emotions to his consciousness.

I love sharing this story with people who assume that I "invented" walk and talk therapy. The fact is that mental health care workers have been walking with their clients for as long as psychotherapy has existed. As clinical regulation became more stringent, this practice was largely done more secretively until 1974, when psychiatrist Thaddeus Kostrubala developed the idea of running with clients as an alternative to standard office-based practice. His success led him to train other practitioners in "running therapy" and to publish a book on the topic. In *The*

Joy of Running, Dr. Kostrubala (1976) talks at length about how running with clients softened the rigid boundaries he'd been taught in the medical model of psychiatry, putting him and the client on a more equal footing (no pun intended) and even making him more likely to share things than he would as a "sitting" psychiatrist. "In this new therapeutic role," Dr. Kostrubala reported, "I was doing something markedly different. I was directly participating in the action with the patient . . . and we experienced similar phenomena—the pain, the high, the altered states" (p. 140).

In my personal running experience, I have felt the runner's high and the dropping of inhibited speech. When I am running with friends, this is less of a concern. However, as a therapist, I am glad that walking does not give me the same endorphin boost that I would get from a harder run. If a therapist were experiencing a release of endorphins leading to a letting down of their guard, they would need to be self-aware enough to discern what is appropriate to say during this unique therapeutic time. Maybe it's a coincidence, or maybe it's a cause and effect, but I've observed that walk and talk therapists tend to be unusually perceptive in seeing clients' whole selves—not simply their issues, but also their strengths—their coping skills and their ability to handle some scenarios quite proficiently even as they struggle with others.

Reading the above passage from Kostrubala, I was struck by the similarity to psychodynamic therapy, an approach that relies on the practitioner's empathic connection with a client's personal perspective. Directly sharing some of the client's struggles in real time—for example, climbing a hill, getting wet in the rain, or traipsing through mud—allows us to model the resilience and awareness that they want to develop. Experiencing adversity and awe alongside them helps to build their understanding that they are not alone but, rather, an important part of this bigger world, leading to a greater capacity for gratitude, grit, and a growth mindset.

Thanks to the vocal support of other early walk and talk therapists (such as Clay Cockrell, Ozzie Gontang, and Kate F. Hays), we have seen a rise since the early 2000s in the number of therapists walking with their clients. Social media groups and the advancement of outdoor adventure therapy (which we'll learn more about in the next chapter) have expanded awareness even further. It's clear that more and more clients are looking for a different type of therapy experience, or at least different options for accessing the care they need. It's also exciting to see how walk and talk meets so many of the demands being raised, from decreased public stigma, to a shift in the therapist-client power dynamics, to more options for the settings and modalities used in the session. All this growth proves that walk and talk isn't something a few therapists just switched to because they were tired of the office. It's meant to be here, right now, to help us reach more people and build a healthier society.

In a way, walk and talk brings us back to the origins of psychotherapy. While it's easy to look back on the early days of our profession and cringe at the indelible images of screaming women and forbidding institutions, the truth is psychoanalysis started by encouraging people to wander freely, both mentally and physically. The meandering mountain path is a literal manifestation of what happens in free association; add physical movement and the unconditional positive regard of the practitioner to the peaceful influence of natural surroundings, and you have a magical combination for constructive openings, new beginnings, creative possibilities, and empowering discoveries.

Chapter 7

Expanding the Horizons of Outdoor Therapy

When I meet someone new and they ask what I do, it's a little challenging to give the ten-second elevator pitch. I usually say something like "I am a psychotherapist, and I walk outside with my clients" or "I combine therapy, nature, and movement in the mental health care process." But as this practice is still unfamiliar to many, I am often met by follow-up questions such as "Oh, is that ecotherapy?" or "Do you work in a wilderness program?"

I don't mind helping clear up this confusion. For me, one of the most exciting things about walk and talk therapy is that it's still in its "toddler" stage. Even as the practice gains momentum, we are continuing to figure out who we are and what makes us different from other nature-based therapies.

That's what this chapter is all about: It helps define a number of therapeutic practices and programs that involve immersion in nature. Some of these programs are just beginning to receive attention, while others are simply the most modern version of a time-honored therapeutic technique. The more we understand what else is out there and why it works, the better we can understand where we fit into the landscape and, better still, improve our own practices with the tools and insights of these other approaches. As you read, ask yourself what these practices contribute to the field of walk and talk, and consider what elements speak to you.

ECOTHERAPY

Ecotherapy, also referred to as nature therapy or green therapy, is the umbrella term for all therapies that integrate nature into mental health counseling. There's no fixed set of rules for what defines ecotherapy. It can range from simply showing the client pictures of nature while sitting in an office, to taking a client into nature for part or all of the therapy session, to even more creative approaches like that of Martin Jordan (2014), author of *Nature and Therapy*, who conducted his therapy sessions in "a willow dome situated within a managed wild garden space" (p. 3). Sometimes the session may focus more on nature than on the client's inner life; other times, the natural space is merely a soothing backdrop for the client's self-exploration. (I bounce between both sides of this spectrum during walk and talk.) Regardless of what form it takes, the goal of ecotherapy is to harness nature's calming, grounding properties to help clients decrease stress, build connections, experience a sense of awe, and develop appreciation for the present moment and the world around them.

Linda Buzzell, a therapist in Santa Barbara and coeditor of *Ecotherapy: Healing with Nature in Mind* (2009), has documented how working with clients outdoors can radically shift the dynamics of the therapy session. "Free of the psychological limits of the small, four-walled, human-built room, a freeing, spacious presence is introduced to the therapy process: more-than-human nature," she told me. "In addition to the issues that have brought the client into therapy (which now have a less-restrictive container), the human-nature relationship itself may become a focus, opening up possible dialogue with the rest of nature and exploration of a wider range of communication and understandings. This bird, this tree, these clouds, this lizard—how might they be relevant to what is happening in the client's life? The spaciousness of open, natural places can also relieve some of the oppression of the client's circumstances, mood, and anxieties, creating new space for exploring alternatives. And fortunately, increasing numbers of research studies are confirming the power of these effects" (personal communication, September 6, 2022).

HORTICULTURE THERAPY

The "roots" of horticulture therapy were established in the early nineteenth century by Dr. Benjamin Rush, a physician known as the "father of American psychiatry." (Fun fact: He was also a signer of the Declaration of Independence.) According to Rutgers University (2022), modern horticultural therapy is defined as "the use of plants and plant-based activity for the purpose of human healing and rehabilitation." While it can often take place in a more formal context, a few therapists I've spoken with incorporate horticulture therapy by simply extending their office space into a backyard garden. Clients can choose to meet in the garden, where they might watch birds and butterflies, plant flowers, pick berries, or forage for mushrooms while they talk. Making these intentional connections with the natural environment leads to openings for conversation about memories from their childhood, self-understanding, or simply feelings of relief or being grounded by the earth. One therapist shared with me how a client, while picking dandelions in their therapy office garden, expressed feeling as if their negative thoughts sometimes needed weeding too. When the therapist pointed out that dandelions are very useful by providing nutrition, flavor, and color, the client was able to look at themselves differently. The dandelion became a metaphor for reframing how to include different parts, rather than eliminate or reject them altogether.

Studies show that clients who engage in horticulture therapy report improved mood, decreased stress, and improved memory. As a person who definitely lacks a green thumb, I'll admit to being a bit skeptical of these claims. That is, until that one time when I did *not* kill an orchid. This feat hardly counts as horticulture—the secret of my success was not touching the soil and continuing to water as directed by the plastic care tag that came with the plant. This went on for an entire year—even after the flowers dropped off, I persisted in hope that my little plant friend might still be alive somewhere in there. Needless to say, I was shocked and beyond excited to see baby buds just a few months later! The visual beauty, the satisfying success, and, most of all, the surprise and awe that came from those new little buds and leaves that arrived seemingly out of nowhere—all those elements were deeply healing to my self-professed title of "plant killer."

While I'm not ready to add this modality to my practice just yet (I'm going to need a few more orchids under my belt before that happens), its therapeutic benefits are clear, especially for people who aren't able to access the outdoors in other ways or for extended periods. Horticulture therapy has been used in community centers, schools, assisted living facilities, and rehabilitation centers to help "improve memory, cognitive abilities, task initiation, language skills, and socialization" (American Horticultural Therapy Association, 2022). I've also seen how this practice can extend to walk and talk. When I'm on the trail with a client, especially a child, I sometimes find myself following them off trail and watching them crouch down to dig in the damp soil, trying to offer some shelter to a fragile sprout or exploring the tangled roots of a large tree. If I'm patient and give them time, they often begin to talk about their feelings with a great deal more candor than when I was asking them questions. Nature speaks to all of us in different ways, and sometimes just putting our hands in the soil can communicate safety, presence, and acceptance of difficult emotions in a way that words cannot.

ANIMAL-ASSISTED THERAPY

Animal-assisted therapy incorporates animals into the therapeutic process. Animals such as dogs, cats, horses, pigs, and birds can complement counseling that is aimed toward the treatment of mood disorders, developmental disabilities, behavioral problems, and more. Animal-assisted therapy is also used in hospital and residential centers to calm clients during difficult moments. This modality can take on many different forms, such as a mental health therapist providing psychotherapy alongside a specially trained animal and, if needed, an animal trainer.

Animal-assisted therapy is often used to help build a client's capacity for empathy, trust, and self-esteem. As with horticulture, there's a particular magic that can happen for some clients when they are put in a "caretaker" role in relation to nature. Some clients find it much easier to connect with an animal than with a person—knowing that the animal will not look shocked, judge them, or say anything critical makes it easier for clients to access and express their emotions. (The unconditional positive regard of the animal is the same as a strict Rogerian therapist!) While incorporating direct contact with animals is a whole modality on its own, animal-assisted therapy can inform walk and talk by reaffirming that an attentive, nonjudgmental, companionable presence can be immensely healing in itself—not to mention the unexpected metaphors provided by occasional animal encounters on the trail! (More on this in chapter 14.)

I was recently walking with a young woman who was dealing with anxiety around a life transition. As we worked to process her ever-changing situation, she mentioned in passing that she grew up riding horses and still rode weekly at a local barn. As she reminisced about caring for her horse when he had an injury, I asked her about what that was like for her. She responded that she really cared about her horse; taking care of him was just like taking care of a friend because of the reciprocal relationship horses have with their riders. "A horse can sense when a person is nervous or is not in a good mood," she said. "We feed off of each other's energy."

I asked this client if she could see any similarities between her time with horses and her experience in walking therapy. "Definitely!" she told me. "The same thing happens when I'm at the barn that happens here. I feel part of a bigger world. I know that I am part of something and that the environment around me is a larger system in which I am living." She went on, "When I ride horses, I have to be completely focused. As someone who has a lot of anxious thoughts, it's really helpful to be so present when riding. When we go out for our therapy walks, I also need to be mindful. We pay attention to the path we're on, and the forest we are walking through, and find ways to connect with the present moment."

WILDERNESS PROGRAMS

Wilderness programs use extended and challenging nature experiences—backcountry treks, camping, use of survival skills over weeks or even months—to treat adolescents and young adults with behavioral or substance abuse problems, especially those who have hit "rock bottom" or endured stints in rehabilitation facilities with no lasting results. Sometimes, taking these clients far from the comforts of modern-day life and the easy access to distraction is the key to helping them confront the emotions and core beliefs driving their negative behavior. The group setting encourages self-discovery hand-in-hand with learning trust and cooperation within a group system, with the end goal of increasing personal identity, self-reliance, positive coping skills, and a sense of belonging.

One teenage client came to me shortly after graduating from a wilderness program. She talked about how she learned strong survival skills and self-reliance both physically and emotionally. We were able to use this experience as a building block for our work— for example, when she began to question a relationship that she had recently begun, we reflected on her time in the wilderness program. When I asked her how she would have handled her conflicting emotions about the relationship during her time in the wilderness, her troubled expression cleared right before my eyes as she reconnected with the techniques she'd learned back then. "I know when something isn't right," she answered. "I'm good at knowing myself. I just need to pay attention to that voice inside of me and feel confident that my voice is enough." Clearly, her time in the wilderness had put her in touch with herself—all she needed was a reminder to invoke that same inner wisdom to guide her life in the "real world."

Just like walking therapy, wilderness programs can make a more lasting impact with some clients than the standard sit-and-talk therapy model. The sensory experiences we enjoy, along with the obstacles and challenges we encounter, leave memorable impressions that are indelibly linked to the internal work we've done. These programs also offer us a chance to live through our fears, teaching us that we are capable of moving through distressing situations and building up our self-esteem through success.

ADVENTURE THERAPY

Adventure therapy uses high-intensity outdoor activities such as rock climbing, rafting, ropes courses, and ziplining to support traditional psychotherapy. Along with enhancing clients' confidence by confronting fears, navigating risk, and mastering skills, adventurous activities like these promote personal growth, support rehabilitation, improve feelings of self-worth, and build trust and communication within a group system. Processing each day's experience through individual or group discussion further instills the skills practiced and lessons learned.

One form of adventure therapy that has always interested me is surf therapy. In a 2021 article titled "Facing the Waves: Therapy in the Surf Circle," clinical psychologists Adam Moss and Nathan Greene share their experience of treating a group of boys challenged by depression, substance abuse, risky behaviors, and trauma. They describe how being in the ocean brought forth a powerful combination of fun, vulnerability, and sensory stimulation that proved a powerful tool for helping the boys better understand themselves.

While walking on a public trail might not feel like an adventure at the same level as ziplining over a rocky valley or dropping into a breaking wave, all these forms of outdoor therapy share one important point: They put the trained psychotherapist in the moment with the client. Experiencing various scenarios on the trail together can't help but build rapport, confidence, and communication within the therapeutic relationship. It also opens the door to "proving" the client's own progress to them. While they might not always be able to see how far they've come in regulating their emotions or staying resilient in the face of conflict, they can look back at a sheer rock face and think, *I climbed that.* A well-trained therapist will utilize these encounters to draw connections between the client's physical accomplishment and the inner strength they're building. For example, "I noticed how you looked a little scared when you saw that steep hill in front of you. I heard you talk about the challenges and consider your reasons for going there. Once you worked through it and actually did the work, I noticed you smiled and seemed to feel a real sense of pride." Then, asking the client to reflect on that experience and expand to other areas in their life, "How might this experience relate to the challenge you are facing in your life right now? What have you learned about yourself?" Practical applications like these are powerful opportunities for growth.

EMPOWERING PRACTITIONERS MEANS EMPOWERING CLIENTS

While evidence has been rolling in regarding the efficacy of outdoor-based therapies, this research is still relatively new, which can make some clinicians still hesitant to engage fully—especially those who work within agencies, schools, and outpatient or intensive treatment centers. How can organizations like these assess the value versus the challenge of utilizing the outdoors as a therapy space?

The fact is that many organizations are already using forms of walking therapy. In some settings, it's a formal program along the lines of those described earlier in the chapter. In others, it happens more spontaneously. I recently spoke with a school counselor who told me about a time when she went for a walk with a student. The counselor stated that there was a very uncomfortable situation that she needed to address with this student. They went for a walk outside around the track. The counselor said that it was helpful for her to be able to walk parallel to the student and discuss the matter at hand. She said that both she and the student were more relaxed while walking, allowing them to brainstorm some creative solutions to the problem. By the time they went back into the building, the mood had shifted, and the student was able to return to class feeling calm.

For this modality to be broadly practicable, there's a lot still to consider. The practices that work for some clients or contexts may not work for others. Every success story is case-dependent, location-dependent, and facility-dependent, at least until practitioners come together to formalize a set of guidelines for outdoor-based therapy across these settings. As longtime health care professionals will tell you, this can often mean that the new idea doesn't go anywhere, at least not for a long time. Now, I admit to being biased, but considering the immense benefits of these different outdoor-based therapy practices, I don't think we can afford to wait! If you're practicing therapy in an institutional or agency setting, start the ball rolling by presenting your supervisors with the evidence-based support for walk and talk. Put your advocacy and internal change skills to work on getting walk and talk approved for use in your organization.

The U.S. Department of Veterans Affairs has learned that veterans with posttraumatic stress disorder (PTSD) can be supported in their healing through experiences in nature. In 2016, a therapeutic nature space called "the Green Road" was constructed on the grounds of Walter Reed National Military Medical Center to serve soldiers returning home from Afghanistan and Iraq. Designed with a wheelchair-accessible path and spaces for memorializing fallen comrades, the Green Road offers a sacred space for veterans to find peace and calm in the presence of a larger and natural world along with moments to reflect.

My time as a social worker has taught me that mental health care workers aren't just clinicians; we're also advocates. Therefore, I believe that those of us in the therapy community need to think carefully about what we are doing and why. Are we trying to maintain the status quo so we can continue our practices with the least amount of friction and inconvenience? Or are we trying to use every method and tool within our power to help people who desperately need mental health support? If it's the latter, exploring options that offer increased flexibility, accessibility, and connection for our clients should be a top priority. The next priority should be validating these options so that practitioners are empowered to use them.

Chapter 8

Walk and Talk for Couples, Families, or Groups

So far, we've focused on how individual therapy works within a walk and talk session. As a result, we haven't spent much time talking about the mechanics of a walking therapy session. With just two people walking and talking, space and attention are almost never an issue. Narrow trail? You can still talk in single file. Challenging moment? It's easy to pause for an emotion to pass or for a mindfulness or breathing exercise to open up new awareness.

While the same benefits we've discussed for individuals—rhythmic movement, mind-body connection, increased creativity, relief from direct eye contact, natural distractions that break up potential tension—are definitely beneficial for couples, families, or other types of groups, walking therapy poses a few more challenges when there's more than one client involved. But as you'll see, if everyone in the session is on board, the benefits can really outweigh the challenges.

COUPLES COUNSELING

While walking with couples, there are a few additional considerations for the therapist to navigate. The most obvious is finding a wide enough path that can accommodate all three people, at least for most of the walk. Obviously, it's not ideal for the therapist to walk with one partner ahead of the other; apart from the message it sends, the last thing you want is for someone to feel left out or not heard. Similarly, if the therapist walks behind the couple for the entire session, they could miss out on important insights or cues from the clients' facial expressions and body language.

This, of course, leads to questions like: Where should the therapist walk in relation to the couple? Is it unfair for the therapist to walk beside one particular member of the couple? Could that be perceived as the therapist choosing sides? On the other hand, is it any better for the therapist to walk in the middle? Is "getting between the couple" a signal of a bad outcome?

Another issue is making sure everyone can be heard during the session. How can you ensure that the conversation is audible to both members of the couple and to the therapist, but not to other people sharing the outdoor space?

Finally, there's the confidentiality issue. More people in the session means more potential for running into an acquaintance. And what if one member of the couple has an emotional moment during the session that makes their partner uncomfortable? While this can always be a factor in couples counseling, being in a public setting like a trail or park has the potential to heighten the discomfort *and* the reaction to that discomfort.

To get some insight from a therapist who has experience working with couples while walking, I spoke with my colleague Tammie Rosenbloom, whom we first met back in chapter 3. Tammie walks with her clients on a paved path around a city lake in Minneapolis. While the serene view helps a lot during couples' walk and talk sessions, Tammie acknowledged that dynamics are always very interesting and ever-shifting, requiring her to pay close attention and move around quite a bit in order to make it work. She described working with one particular couple, whom she had walk next to each other while she moved aside. Whenever their discussion began to escalate into a fight, she stepped back in to offer tools that helped them work through the issue, then she continued walking behind them while they practiced these new skills together. Taking into consideration all these moving parts, the couple chose to continue with Tammie outdoors, even through the freezing cold winter. By the end, the couple thanked Tammie and said how helpful it had been to do counseling outdoors while walking.

Ultimately, there's no way around it: Walk and talk couples therapy is a little more complicated than an individual session. Still, the benefits can definitely be worth the extra effort. Be transparent with your couples clients about the need for trial and error in your first few sessions as you all figure out together what works best in terms of distance, pace, positioning, and so on. Switch things up as you go—let your instincts guide you in moving from one side of the couple to the other, or to the middle, or even behind them occasionally. Communicate about what you're doing and check in with the couple throughout the session to see how it's working for them.

FAMILY THERAPY

Many of the same issues we discussed about walking therapy with couples also apply to family therapy in the outdoors. Depending on the size of the family group and the ages of the children, this might be an excellent place to build in some of the other outdoor therapeutic practices outlined in chapter 7. For example, for families with young children, you might start a session at a picnic table in a park, then move on to the playground, where you can observe the interactions of family members. Another idea might be to start on a blanket under a tree, then initiate a group activity like collecting flowers or seashells or building a sandcastle or a rock tower. For families with older children, a group hike or a team-building activity can be another great option. It all depends on the object of the therapy and the goal.

Family therapist Lauri Flick-Harty, who practices in Delafield, Wisconsin, shared a great story with me about what an outdoor family counseling session can achieve. Lauri practices walk and talk therapy on the trails of Lapham Peak, a state park with some of the most variable terrain imaginable—as she describes it, "smooth and paved, rocky and hilly, winding through woods and meadows. And of course, in Wisconsin there can be terrific warmth and sunshine or snowy, icy cold weather" (personal communication, May 4, 2022). Compared to practicing in an office, Lauri sees walking family therapy as a unique opportunity to transcend limiting patterns. For many months, she worked with a family of five—two parents and three young adult children—that was plagued by loss and conflict. In office sessions, each family member competed to be heard. There were raised voices, interruptions, and talking over each other, or else stony silence with arms crossed over chests. However, says Lauri, "From our first trail session, a different family appeared. At first, the novelty of the park as a therapy setting seemed to disrupt their usual reactive behavioral patterns. Quite naturally then, walking and talking and taking in nature seemed to encourage turn-taking in their conversation. They verbally expressed reverence and appreciation of the natural world, and this attitude spread to how they treated each other. They asked each other questions. They seemed to listen more carefully. My most frequent intervention was punctuating and extending the positive activity that was happening" (personal communication, May 4, 2022).

As Lauri adjusted to outdoor sessions, she felt that her therapeutic skills and the natural environment combined to create a holding and healing space where the family's best selves could emerge. "It's been some time since that first Lapham visit with the family," she added, "but I believe some of those interpersonal patterns have continued in a changed and positive way."

Here are a few important tips for starting a walk and talk family session:

- Don't offer a trail session for a family's first therapy session. It's important to assess safety and even compatibility with the elements before taking a family group outdoors. Use the first session or two to see how the group interacts with each other and to get a sense of the different family members' readiness for an outdoor session.

- If you think walk and talk would be a good option for a family, or if someone in the family expresses interest, offer the option to the entire family at the same time: "What if we meet outside next time? How would that be for each of you?" Getting consent from everyone, even minor children, will be important for a productive walk and talk session. (You'll also need informed consent signed by everyone.)

- Make sure to impress on the parents that they'll need to come prepared with anything their group might need, especially if there are young children involved. (You as the therapist can't bring enough water bottles for everyone.) Also, talk to the parents about preparing their kids for the excursion, emphasizing the importance of staying together and keeping to the designated trail.

- Since family sessions tend to take longer than the usual fifty-minute session, ensure that you're choosing a trail that is doable for the ages and ability levels of everyone in the family for that length of time. If there are young kids, I highly recommend a setting with plenty of public bathrooms, places to sit down, and even a play structure or other kid-friendly amenities.

- Lauri acknowledges that it can be a challenge sometimes to hear everyone during the session, depending on each member's position and the sounds of the outdoor environment. The upshot is that sometimes she asks people to take more care with their speech—never a bad thing, especially in a therapy context!

GROUP THERAPY

Along with providing a welcome alternative to a dingy meeting room, outdoor group therapy offers the benefits of any ecotherapy model: creativity, open-minded thinking, a connection to nature, and closeness to others in a shared space and activity. Here's the template I've developed to adapt individual walking therapy to a group setting:

- I begin with an introduction to the day's activity while the group is seated together in an open setting. I let them know what to expect and how the session is going to work—how long we'll be walking, what we'll be talking about, what my co-facilitator and I will be doing during the walk, what they can expect when we pause for a group exercise, and so forth.

- Depending on the group, I might lay down some ground rules myself or let them establish their own rules via group discussion. Two important things to emphasize are (1) observing trail etiquette (e.g., staying together, not venturing off the trail) and (2) protecting each other's privacy (e.g., no texting, photo taking, or social media sharing of the session, even after we all go home).

- To facilitate discussion on the trail, I break the group up into smaller groups or pairs. Depending on the topic or the goal of the day's session, I sometimes find it useful to pass out "cheat sheets" so they don't forget the questions. Other times, it's fine to simply brief the group on the questions ahead of time, then give them cues to move from one topic to the next as we go.

- I utilize the natural conditions of the trail or the outdoor environment to incorporate mindfulness-based practices. Of course, some participants may use these breaks in the walk to talk amongst themselves or focus on distractions. When this happens, I will sometimes acknowledge it and ask them to share what they are noticing, thereby turning their distraction into a focus that serves the whole group. Other times, I might give the distracted person a "job" to get them involved—this tends to work well with younger folks who need a physical application for their energy.

- When the session draws to a close, I bring the group back to the area where we began so that we can summarize what we've done and end with a sense of togetherness.

Some of my biggest successes in group therapy have been with teens. Surprised? Let me tell you about the Teen Mindfulness Group we held while hiking a beautiful trail that ran along a creek. It was me, two co-facilitators, ten middle-school-age kids, and three trained therapy dogs (and their owners) from a local pet therapy program. The kids took a liking to the dogs immediately and were very responsive to the "dog moms'" instructions for how the dogs like to be approached. After my initial welcome and icebreaker (name, favorite animal, goals they wanted to get out of the session), the kids continued to interact with the dogs while I led a discussion on anxiety. We had a group conversation about how anxiety affects your body—discussing familiar topics like panic attacks and fight-or-flight reactions—then explored some of the mindful breathing techniques that can help with those responses.

Next, we headed out on our hike! Along the way, we interspersed the mindfulness exercises we'd introduced earlier and talked about what the teens noticed, how they felt, and how to hold a feeling without reacting. We practiced the five senses exercise (described in chapter 3) and discussed what they observed.

Traditionally, a group therapy session would include stopping for a group discussion. But because I wanted the kids to receive the benefits of hiking, I had them partner up for mini-discussion groups as we continued on the trail. They took turns asking each other questions about their worries, how those worries affected their life, how they might change their way of thinking, and what ideas or resources could support them. Next, I had them switch partners and again take turns asking each other new questions that focused on coping strategies. Finally, as the hike was ending, I asked them to walk the last five minutes in silence to just observe both their surroundings and what they were feeling inside. When we returned to the trailhead, the kids concluded the session by sitting on benches, briefly processing what had been helpful, and writing new ideas down in their journals before saying goodbye.

Thinking back to this session made me smile—I loved working with this group! It was invigorating to see a group of middle schoolers, usually shy and anxious to share, open up easily, smile, and move their bodies. I felt a sense of calm as I watched them breathe and relax in nature. I also felt their attention was greater than groups I have run for the same population indoors. There is something about the freedom to be slightly distracted on the trail that keeps things natural and unclenched. Of course, keeping distraction and freedom in the "beneficial zone" requires a little extra effort on the therapist's side.

Here are some recommendations for a successful outdoor group therapy session. Keep in mind that there are a lot of overlapping principles here that coincide with successful indoor therapy groups:

- **Prepare well.** On my advertising flyer, I clearly stated the focus of the group, as well as the target age and audience (middle schoolers with some history of anxiety). The flyer included the fact that therapy dogs would be present, preparing potential group members for this situation. I then screened each person by having a thorough phone call with their parent. I asked about their experience hiking, walking, exposure to outdoors, and any health concerns.

- **Bring a co-facilitator.** Co-facilitators are really important to me when leading larger groups for walk and talk. A co-facilitator serves many roles: helping with check-in, wrangling people on the trail, aiding in emergencies, keeping me on schedule, and adding their valuable contributions during the group. Not to mention, it's great to debrief with your partner after the session!

- **Know what you're getting yourself into.** It's extra important to check the trail out ahead of time with your specific group in mind. Be mindful of conditions the day of, in case there are obstacles or weather conditions that may make it more difficult. I recommend taking a quick hike or bike ride along the trail prior to the session.

- **Find an icebreaker that sets the right tone.** The kids in this group did not know each other outside of this group, but they instantly bonded over their affection for the dogs. Along with helping the participants open up and engage, these calm, well-behaved dogs (and their dog moms) played an important role in setting a tone that communicated "all are welcome, and judgment is not present."

- **Use the movement to your advantage.** If you've ever led a group activity indoors (or just played a round of musical chairs), you know how awkward it can be to watch participants find their place or choose a partner. In contrast, when we walked on the trail and kids were paired together, I noticed a general letting go of inhibition. There was no pressure to perform or to look directly at one another; the safety of side-by-side movement seemed to help them open up more easily. When we stopped for mindfulness breaks or to change partners, already being on their feet translated to remarkable ease in finding someone new with whom to begin sharing.

- **Be a full participant, not just an observer.** My co-facilitator and I toggled back and forth between walking with someone to answer the reflection questions or joining a duo to participate in their discussion. It's valuable for the therapist to serve as a role model, showing kids how to share anxious thoughts and work on them through discussion. (I kept my examples relatable and not too personal.)

I have dreams of doing all different kinds of therapy groups on the trail: with young adults struggling to find their way, moms experiencing postpartum depression, bereaved partners and families working through their grief, cancer patients or survivors, and more. The combination of nature, movement, and therapy offers unlimited potential for finding relief, validation, and inspiration. So do your planning, lace up your boots, and invite participants to move alongside you as you do your best work yet.

Spring:

Nurturing the Seeds of
Your Walk and Talk Practice

" There is something infinitely healing in the repeated refrains of nature—the assurance that dawn comes after night, and spring after winter. "

–Rachel Carson

Chapter 9

How to Maintain Professionalism Outside

Before any TV show begins taping, the stage crew is behind the scenes setting the lights, organizing the costumes, wiring the microphones, and placing the cameras. In a similar way, a therapist begins each session before the client even arrives. For us, setting the "stage" means establishing a structure that provides safety for the client and determines the expectations and boundaries necessary for this unique working relationship to flourish. The therapeutic frame—which includes elements such as the role of the therapist, the space, the time, fees, and communicating your policies on cancellations and rescheduling—is all about setting expectations for what you'll be doing in the session and how it might feel for them. This provides a sense of caring professionalism and reliability that is foundational for effective therapy.

PREPARING FOR YOUR SESSION

If you've been a therapist for any length of time, you likely have your office setup routine down to a science. Consequently, one of the biggest questions you might have is how to set the stage for a session without an office. For me, it starts as soon as a prospective client calls.

INTAKE CALL

When a potential client reaches out to me for therapy, I make sure that I schedule uninterrupted time to talk with them on the phone. After all, this is where the therapeutic relationship begins—I want them to see and feel that they have my attention for the time we spend together. The lack of interruption is also important for me, as this call is my opportunity to make sure my practice is a good fit for them—and I don't just mean the walking. Along with hearing their story about what is motivating them to seek therapy, my goal during this call is to assess what their needs may be at a deeper level so I can consider how to best accommodate them in our work together.

I usually start by asking the prospective client how they got my name. Their answer often tells me if they are already familiar with my way of practicing therapy. Even if they are aware of the walk and talk aspect, I go over the basic details with them and ask about their comfort level around having a session in a public outdoor space. This leads to me discussing privacy, location, timing, and weather. I also take this opportunity to ask about their physical health—what kind of exercise they typically do and how often, any health conditions or injuries I should be aware of, and any restrictions or limitations advised by their physician. (This isn't the last time I'll assess the client's physical health, as you'll see in a moment.)

Once we've covered the walk and talk of it all, I ask a few other screening-related questions that are typical for therapists to inquire about: what brings you to therapy, have you been to therapy before, are you seeing any other mental health professionals, and so on. If signs point to a good match, we find a mutually agreed upon time and location to meet for our first session together.

INFORMED CONSENT

> *If you skipped through the whole book to get to this part, I'm not hurt. I've been consulted by a lot of beginning walk and talk therapists who are mainly interested in this information so they can check the regulatory boxes and get out on the trail. I applaud your enthusiasm, but now that you're about to get what you came for, I encourage you to visit other sections of this book and read more about everything that goes into a successful walk and talk session.*

The informed consent is a written agreement between the therapist and client that establishes the relevant facts of your working relationship. When therapists write an informed consent, we take into account our professional ethical obligations (determined by our licensing board and professional association), privacy concerns, and the safety of the client. We also consider our own professional roles and our limitations as individual practitioners with our own specific vision and values. And then we try to cram it all in there while keeping the language simple and clear. I strongly recommend that you consult with a lawyer, your malpractice insurance, and your licensing board to cover all your bases, then go back and rewrite an informed consent that is clear, conversational, and free of legalese. It's worth noting that my professional malpractice insurance plan generally covers me for my professional therapy advice and only sometimes for physical office space. As plans vary, it's important to find out the exact details of your plan and how it will apply to an outdoor setting.

The following are the main topics you'll want to include in your own informed consent. To help ensure the client reads and affirms their understanding of each item, I recommend adding a short, underlined space like this _____ to each line for initials.

- Your professional limitations to your confidentiality, privacy, and HIPPA (given that you are outside where you may be seen).

- A disclaimer and notice of the client's responsibility for their own health and safety during the sessions. You can include a line about them being responsible for their personal property as well.

- What is and isn't your role as a mental health care provider. Basically, you want to make it clear that you're a mental health care provider, not a personal trainer or a physical therapist.

- A description of the setting, risk factors, and liability concerns with exercise and outdoors.

- Any additional issues your malpractice insurance provider recommends regarding coverage while walking outdoors.

- A liability waiver. If you are trained in first aid or CPR, consider adding a clause about that here. Ideally, you'll consult with a lawyer in crafting this part.

After the client has signed the form, review these items (again) with them and ask if they have any questions. If you sense hesitancy or confusion on their part, explore the reasons and determine if in-office or telehealth sessions might be more appropriate for now. Remember, walk and talk is an option well-suited for certain people *and* for certain stages of treatment.

THE "GOOD FIT" ASSESSMENT

As mentioned earlier, you'll want to ask some questions during your intake call about the client's general physical health. I recommend explaining right up front that you have this talk with everyone as a precautionary measure so that you better understand how best to guide the session.

I start with asking about the client's general health: Do they have any specific conditions I should know about (joint pain, injury-prone areas, breathing problems, etc.)? Do they take any medications? Are they seeing a physician regularly? Then I ask about their exercise habits in a general way. I don't need to know their weight or their resting heart rate, but I do need to know how comfortable they are with sustained low-impact physical activity. I typically ask what their exercise habits look like and what their recent experience has been regarding walking, hiking, and running.

The biggest insights, though, will happen in your first session. Check in with the client as soon as you meet up—ask how they're feeling and if they're ready to go, and keep your awareness keen for any sign of discomfort. As you walk, observe how they look, how they move, and especially how they breathe.

Paying attention to my client's breath gives me so much information. Are we going too fast, or not fast enough? Does speaking about stressful events change their breathing pattern, and what do they notice about their own breathing?

If you have a concern, communicate it! Most health-related concerns can be worked out, like the client who carried excess weight and was very determined to improve his health, both physically and mentally. As soon as we'd hit the trail, he was off like a rocket—I struggled to keep up with him. But after covering a mile and a half in twenty minutes, he'd be exhausted by the pace he'd kept, and it would take us twice as long to get back. After a couple of sessions like this, I explained to him the benefit of moderating our pace so that we could get the most out of the session. (I also started having us turn around a bit earlier, just in case we were up against the clock.) Talk honestly with the client about what you're noticing and work with them to find a mutual solution. This not only aids the session, but also gives the client insight into their own activity level and what that means to them.

In general, walk and talk is pretty self-selecting. People who wouldn't be a good fit for it usually don't seek it out. Still, I've learned from experience to recognize when walk and talk isn't a good option for someone at that time. If they have a recent history of erratic or harmful behavior, I personally would not walk and talk with them until they have made some measurable progress. If someone is fitting therapy into a very tight schedule, they also might not be a good fit—pacing while walking isn't an exact science, and nature has a talent for causing unexpected delays. Trickier to spot, though, are the people for whom meeting outside of an office means meeting on their terms instead of yours. They might want to change their usual time slot or ask you to meet at a trail that's more convenient for them. I'll admit that when I was first getting started, I often accommodated situations like these because, well, I wanted to fill my caseload. It didn't take long, though, to realize what we always realize when we stretch our boundaries: It often leads to resentment, which makes it impossible to do our best work. As the therapist, you must be in charge of the session, and that includes selecting the best trail for therapy. After all, the client wouldn't ask you to change the location of your office.

How do you recognize boundary pushers on the intake call? My best advice is to listen for cues about their expectations. We all learn over time how to recognize people who are ready to schedule a therapy session but not really commit to the work involved. Use your best judgment and give people a chance. Sometimes they just need time and space to get used to this new idea, whether that is walk and talk or therapy in general.

YOUR OUTDOOR "OFFICE"

With those foundational pieces in place, the next part of the therapeutic frame is creating a safe space to do the work. When you are providing therapy in an office, you have a responsibility to keep your office clean and safe. Needless to say, practicing outside requires you to think about safety in a different way. The following are a few precautions to consider for the client's physical safety out on the trail.

SCOUTING A LOCATION

When choosing where to walk for a therapy session, it probably goes without saying that you need to look for routes and settings that are first and foremost comfortable for the client. Remember, everyone is different, both in their physical strength and their bandwidth for the inherent unpredictability of the outdoors. I have some adventurous clients who love a good climb through virtually untouched wilderness. Other clients prefer a paved path that hugs the edges of the "civilized world," offering easy access to streets in case of an emergency. Regardless of how easy or challenging the terrain of your walk, I encourage you to know where you are going, have your "safety exit" routes identified, and be prepared to direct an ambulance to your location in case of an emergency.

If an urban walk sounds like an easy way to circumvent these concerns . . . well, not so fast. The city can be as unpredictable and obstacle-ridden as any nature trail.

Whether you're walking on a city street, in an urban park or greenway, or even through a quiet neighborhood, you can encounter issues like traffic, construction, neighbors, crowds, and noise. And while you're less likely to encounter wildlife or fallen branches, you'll still have to be vigilant on your client's behalf for intersection crossings, distracted drivers, and the presence of other pedestrians. While I'm not saying walk and talk can only be done in nature, it's worth noting that my colleagues have confirmed that an urban walk can bring a lot more distractions—nothing derails a session like finding your client engaged in some "accidental" window shopping along the way.

So how do you properly assess a potential site for walk and talk? You walk it! In fact, my colleague Denice Crowe Clark recommends visiting the location on different days of the week and at different times of day to get a feel for the level of foot traffic. Ideally, you want a path that is well-enough traveled that you feel safe taking clients there, but not so crowded that it would be detrimental to the session's confidentiality or the client's comfort with speaking freely. Make note of landmarks such as restrooms, water fountains, park benches, shelters, and areas where people tend to gather. As you walk the trail, keep your eyes open for options that let you add distance when a client walks more rapidly, or take a shortcut or turnaround for clients who walk slowly. Depending on the setting, you may also want to think about the unhoused folks who might spend time in the park or nature preserve you've chosen. Even though these folks are unlikely to interfere with you, some clients are uncomfortable around them and may need to consider their presence before agreeing to a walk and talk session. It's also worth keeping up with neighborhood watch pages so that you'll have advance notice if there have been recurring issues with individuals interacting in unpleasant ways with park visitors. Needless to say, if something like this comes to your attention, you'll want to alter your route until the problem has been resolved.

Finally, you want to learn the path well enough that, should there be an emergency, you can direct medical personnel to your location. As you walk, take a pause here and there and practice how you might identify that exact spot to an ambulance driver—for example, "the northeast corner of the park near the splash pad."

If it sounds like a lot of work, well, it is. Denice Crowe Clark confirms that walking therapy "requires a particular amount of presence to multiple processes and attention to the frame of outdoor therapy" (personal communication, May 10, 2022). But don't let that deter you—this type of awareness becomes second nature over time and with practice.

CHECKING THE WEATHER

There are two levels of consideration when it comes to the weather. The first is the practical issue of how the elements will impact the session. The second is the analogous relationship between the weather and the client's mood, and how weather can be an asset to the therapy session (more on that ahead).

First let's discuss the practical issue of the elements: Is there anything about the day's weather that presents a prohibitive risk to your client's safety? This isn't just a matter of whether there's a lightning storm or a record heat wave. If they have asthma, could the cold air on a winter day irritate their lungs? Will a light sprinkle cause their arthritis to flare? Before each session, ask yourself whether, given what you have learned about your client's fitness level, the weather presents any practical limitation to your client's ability to participate safely in their therapy.

On days when the answer is yes, you're not necessarily relegated to the traditional chair-in-office setting. Tammie Rosenbloom has found a clever workaround for sessions in her northern climate: "When the winter temperatures and icy conditions make it difficult to walk in January, I offer virtual sessions instead. Sometimes clients will walk on their home treadmills while we have a session over the phone" (personal communication, May 9, 2022). Another therapist said she does not allow treadmill telehealth sessions because she gets dizzy watching the client bounce around on the video.

It's important to consider not just today's weather, but yesterday's as well. As Denice Crowe Clark writes, "On more than one occasion, after high winds or a big storm, I have gone out and found trees uprooted or large branches fallen. As a result, I choose to change routes or opt to reschedule sessions when winds are high or after particularly heavy rains" (personal communication, May 10, 2022).

It should go without saying, but if there's a hindrance to your client's ability to safely walk and talk at the same time, they can't participate meaningfully in their therapy. As the therapist, it's often up to you to make this call. (And you'd be surprised how hard it can be to talk a client out of their walking therapy session once they get into it!) Even if your client is enthusiastic about still having their session outdoors, it's your responsibility to remind them that the goal of the walk is their therapy session, and it's not easy to have a talk when you're navigating your way through a washed-out trail or trying to outrun an oncoming storm.

PREPARING THE CLIENT (WHAT TO WEAR AND BRING)

One day, a client of mine showed up to a walk and talk session in flip-flops, leaving me confused. What happened? She'd walked with me before, but never in such flimsy footwear. What to do?

Since I didn't have an extra pair of sneakers, I made a snap decision to just go with the flow. We took the trail at a much slower pace than usual, and I made a mental note to talk with her afterward about the importance of bringing proper shoes for our sessions. Halfway through the walk, though, she revealed the reason she was wearing flip-flops: a midnight swim at her ex's house, followed by a "sleepover," both of which set off a small crisis for the client, as she'd recently vowed to avoid such escapades. Being a bit embarrassed by both the shoes and the reason behind them ended up making her *very* receptive to the day's session. (I noticed that going forward, she always wore supportive shoes.)

I wish that all walk and talk wardrobe malfunctions were as understandable as that one. One time, a client showed up in his bedroom slippers! It seems he'd forgotten that we'd be walking outside. On a dirt path. During the onset of winter. Then there are the clients who show up in high heels. (Oy, the heels . . .) Why? There is *always* a reason. The last time I encountered this, the client had just come from a work meeting that had run late, giving her no time to change into sneakers. Her shoes were the least of her worries at that moment—she was still seething from the way she'd been treated at the meeting. When I offered to sit on the park bench for our session, she said that she'd rather blow off steam by walking. We made it ten minutes before she slipped the shoes off and carried them the rest of the way. Since it was warm outside, I decided to follow suit, and we took advantage of the opportunity to ground ourselves through the connection of our bare feet with the earth.

While footwear snafus can make for good stories and sometimes even good sessions, that said, your client's safety demands that you emphasize the importance of wearing outdoor-appropriate shoes. If they have (or discover) specific bodily concerns related to walking, such as plantar fasciitis or weak joints, they have options to continue with supportive socks, shoe inserts or orthotics, a knee or ankle brace—whatever they need to keep themselves safe and healthy.

The same rules extend to clothing, which can be even easier to get wrong than shoes. There is a famous Norwegian saying attributed to Sir Ranulph Fiennes that goes something like this: "There is no such thing as bad weather, only bad clothing." I have learned Sir Ranulph's point the hard way, having been caught underprepared in rain, cold, and heat more often than I'd like to admit. Once I finally invested in a long winter coat and hiking boots that could handle the snow and mud puddles, I felt much more relaxed and comfortable during winter walking sessions. Since then, I've collected all sorts of gear tailored to different types of weather. My wide-brimmed straw hat, lightly tinted sunglasses (that leave my eyes still visible to my walking partner), and lightweight shoes make the summer heat more manageable, while my tall rain boots, heavy-duty raincoat, and large clear umbrella make rainy walks a lot more fun than they used to be. And, of course, my tried-and-true layering approach to dressing ensures that I'm ready for any sudden change in temperature.

Having learned all this, you can be sure I offer the same advice to my clients as well. Some are quicker than others to follow it. I watched one young man walk throughout the fall and winter with me with his hands shoved deep into his sweatshirt pockets. Even as the winter edged on, a mere sweatshirt seemed to keep him warm. Meanwhile, I was dressed in my parka, wool hat, mittens, boots, and scarf. I never commented, but I did watch him adjust his wardrobe as the weeks went on. One particularly brisk day, he showed up with two sweatshirts on! The next week, he added a vest, and the following week, gloves. In general, unless a client arrives wearing something that could be harmful for their safety on the trail, I leave it to them to consider their own needs and simply lead by example when it comes to shoes, clothes, and gear.

> *Fact: A water bottle can be handy for walk and talk sessions, and not only for drinking in the hot summer months. You never know if you may need to splash water on your face, rinse pollen out of your nose or dust out of your eyes, or cool off a sting from an insect. Also, you will get thirsty. Bring the water.*

SELF-CARE FOR THE WALKING THERAPIST

Now that we've covered the major safety considerations for your client, let's talk about how to ensure *your* safety as the provider.

ASSESSING THE CLIENT'S RESILIENCE

The outdoors is inherently unpredictable, and for some clients, that alone can be a drawback. Your client may have every indication of physical fitness, but based on your interaction with them, do they seem mentally and emotionally resilient enough for this new therapy setting? To be blunt, will they want to sue you every time they stub their toe on a tree root, or can they be resilient and take this sort of thing in stride? (No pun intended.) Constant assessment is the name of the game. If at any point you or your client need to change paths, initiate that conversation with them right away. Here's a little script to help you along:

> "Is this working for you? It seems that you've been really nervous about talking in this space. Would you like to try meeting virtually or in the office next time?"

ACCOUNTABILITY AND CHECK-INS

I remember arriving at the trail one time with a feeling of . . . uncertainty, shall we say? . . . about the new client I was about to meet. This young man had provided little information about himself on our brief phone call, saying he'd prefer to share in person. While there weren't any obvious warning signs, knowing a little less about the client than usual lit up those "being a female in the outdoors" alert centers in my brain. So I did what I always do, and sent my usual check-in text to my husband: "Hi. I'm about to meet a new client at the park. I'll text you when I'm done at 11:00. If you don't receive my post-session message, come find my body in the woods."

To be clear, the ominous tone of the text is an ongoing joke between my husband and me. (If I had any real feeling that this session might end with a body in the woods, I wouldn't have booked it.) Having accountability while you're out in nature is a basic safety measure for a person of any gender, and that doubles when you're meeting a stranger for a walk. Think through the concerns you or your family might have, make (and follow) a safety plan, let your people know where you'll be and when, and most importantly, always trust your gut. It's better to change plans, even if it means looking unprofessional, than to risk your personal safety.

Oh, you want to know how that session turned out? When I met him in person, I instantly saw that this client read as shy rather than secretive. He warmed up quickly on the trail and shared about many personal vulnerabilities, as well as his feelings of sadness over the death of a close family member. I could tell he really needed to talk, and I felt that we had a great first session. Returning to my car, I glanced up while texting my husband "I am alive and well" and saw my client feeding the geese and birds from a box of Cheerios. I couldn't help but smile, both at the touching sight and at the sweet proof that I had worried for nothing.

HAVE A PLAN (OR THE TRAINING) FOR ACCIDENTS

The amount of emergency preparedness training you can seek out can run the gamut, and it really depends on your goals for walking therapy. Some walk and talk therapists choose to get first aid or CPR training to keep in their back pocket in case of emergencies. In my view, even if you're doing walk and talk in a local park (as opposed to in "the wild"), this type of training can only be beneficial for you and your client. It's a short investment in time and money that can help put your mind at ease and improve your confidence in isolated or tricky settings.

Other therapists choose to simply bring along a few bandages, alcohol pads, or other small supplies that could be helpful on the trail. Personally, I have carried the same two bandages in my bag for five years of walk and talk and have never used them. You know what I could have used, though? A set of tweezers when a bee stung me.

It's important to know that you are *not* required by law to attend to an emergency, regardless of any training or preparation you do or don't have. (Don't let that final episode of *Seinfeld* scare you.) Furthermore, all U.S. states have a "Good Samaritan" law that protects people from criminal charges when they are trying to assist someone during an emergency. All that to say, you're not legally liable either way. But regardless of what you choose to do, I recommend putting language in your informed consent that draws a line between your responsibility and the client's during the session.

Finally, if you do find yourself in a situation to use emergency skills, make sure you ask the injured person directly if they'd like your assistance (taking into account their state of consciousness). People have vastly different personal boundaries when it comes to touch, and the same rules around touch that you would follow in the therapy office also apply in the outdoors. The exception, of course, is if the client is in imminent danger or unresponsive—in that situation, you may do what needs to be done to protect your client's safety and save a life. It's also a good idea to make a plan with the client about how you'll deal with emergency personnel in the unlikely event that you have to call them. Let them know the circumstances under which you'd make the decision to call for help and ask if they have a preference about whether or not you identify yourself as their therapist to paramedics or police. You can even put this into your informed consent so that everyone is in agreement ahead of time.

If you choose not to get training in first aid or other emergency skills, you'll want to take extra care in familiarizing yourself with the route you're on and the surrounding area. Keep a note handy that describes places where emergency personnel can access the trail, and have a plan in mind about where and how you'd go about getting help if you needed it.

PREPARING FOR THE UNPREDICTABLE

Ironically, having a background in anxiety (both professionally and personally), I can list all the concerns that have true potential to become a reality during a walk and talk session. Environmental concerns can be anything from poorly cleared or maintained trails (branches in the face, tree roots underfoot, mud or loose stones slipping us up— oh my!) to disasters like forest fires or flash floods. What if insects fly out and startle or bite us as we walk? What if we have an encounter with a snake or another wild animal? (Or, for that matter, a badly behaved domesticated animal?)

Then there are the human error factors. What if the client snags their favorite jacket on a branch? What if they get a blister halfway through the walk? What if you get back to the parking lot and realize somebody dropped their wallet or left their phone behind? I could go on, but you get the idea.

What can you do to prevent these things from happening? Not a whole lot. Nature is wild, which is part of its allure. (And, I believe, its benefit for therapy.) Before you decide to trade in this walk and talk idea for simply hanging a nice landscape photo on your office wall, remember that your new informed consent is designed expressly to cover your liability in this setting. Once you've summarized safety concerns and asked the client to assume responsibility for their own safety and personal property, your role is simply to advise, remind, and occasionally make the call when plans need to change. Make it easy for yourself by downloading an hour-by-hour weather app so you can keep an eye on conditions and give the client a heads-up if any special preparation (a raincoat, extra layers, mud-friendly shoes) is needed.

With all the necessary focus on preparing your client for comfort and safety, it's sometimes easy to forget your own comfort as well. I went into walking therapy partly because I'm pretty open to walking in just about any weather. If that's not you, it's okay to limit your walking sessions to certain times of year or certain conditions on the trail. Just keep in mind that you'll need to communicate these boundaries to your client up front *and* stick to your commitment within those boundaries. Some clients may come to really value meeting outside, and if you change your plan at the last minute, they will be disappointed. Part of the therapeutic frame is honoring the commitment you've made, even when it's uncomfortable.

THE THERAPIST IS THE LEADER

Leading the way is a very important part of your role as a walking therapist. It allows the client to invest in their therapy—not having to stay alert to their surroundings lets them focus on their story and their feelings. As the client talks, I direct their steps when necessary by gently pointing when we are about to make a turn or when there's a puddle, rock, or root in their path. By gesturing, I avoid needing to interrupt the client as they're talking or thinking.

Being the leader also means that you must keep an eye on the time. Until you get used to your new route, keep a watch handy. I prefer a simple analog watch that won't distract me with apps, texts, or phone calls. Keep in mind that coming back usually takes longer than going out. A colleague of mine finds it helpful to set a vibrating alarm to alert her halfway through the session when it's time to turn around.

THE CLIENT SETS THE PACE

Even though you are leading the way, the client is the one who should determine the pace. During your first session with a client, check in with them every so often to see if they are comfortable with the speed and intensity of your walk. Paying attention to how they are breathing and how easily they're able to speak will also give you a good clue. Keep in mind that not only is each person's preferred pace different, but their mental health and emotional state will also be a factor. As you might expect, clients struggling with depression tend to walk much more slowly than those dealing with anxiety. Clients may also pause their walking to finish a thought or just be with a heavy emotion. While wearing your therapy hat, keep in mind how to gently move them along when they're ready to press "play" again.

WEATHERING THE WEATHER

As I mentioned earlier, there are two levels of consideration regarding the weather. Now that we've gone over the practical, safety-focused perspective, let's look at how unexpected weather can be an asset to the therapy session.

Over the years of practicing walk and talk, I've come to see weather as a complete metaphor for life. The comparison is almost too obvious: Just like life, weather and nature are not in our control. Some days are sunny, some are a bit cloudy, some are dark and moody. We go through seasons where every day is warm and inviting, followed by seasons of bitter cold or punishing heat. And sometimes the weather is just downright flaky, making it impossible to predict what we'll need to keep us safe and comfortable.

These metaphors can be priceless during a therapy session. No matter the outdoor conditions, we can find a connection to our emotions that makes them more understandable, along with a living analogy for the coping skills that help us persevere through hard times. Rainy days teach us that we can choose to endure. Oppressive heat pushes us to breathe, move slowly, and take breaks in the face of difficulty. If we can successfully hold the therapeutic frame by maintaining resilience and confidence, seasonal fluctuations and unexpected weather events remind us that we are part of a bigger world where changes can happen with no warning and that we can have different feelings about them while ultimately learning to accept them.

· · · · ·

Jake has proved to be truly committed to his therapy process—he shows up no matter what. As the weather begins warming up, I gently suggest that we can always do a telehealth session in extreme weather. Not once does he take me up on the offer.

On this day, the temperature is over eighty degrees. I've only been at the trailhead a few minutes and already I'm dripping with sweat, yet there he is, pulling into his parking spot right on time. I admit to faltering for a moment—*why did I think this outdoor-based practice was such a good idea again?* Nevertheless, we exchange our usual nod of greeting and head off down the trail.

Jake begins by catching me up on life: pretty good week at work, weekend trip to the beach, kids had a great time swimming in the ocean. Eventually, I ask, "Was this your first vacation without your wife?"

"Yes," he admits. "That part was really sad. I think we all felt her absence, especially the first day or so. I asked the kids what they wanted to do with their feelings about missing her. You know what they said? They wanted to build a fire at night, write notes to her, and put them in the fire."

"Wow, how clever! They came up with that?"

"Yes! And that is exactly what we did. We built the fire, talked a lot about her, and even talked about our feelings. There were some tears." He pauses to gather himself. "Then we wrote the notes and threw them into the fire."

"How was that for you, Jake?"

After a long silence, he answers, "I felt good about it. Look, nothing will ever be the same, but what we did do is grieve as a family. We took time to be together, talk, and acknowledge one another's feelings. I think we opened up more than we ever have, and that felt pretty darn good." He goes on, "The rest of the week, I think we felt a little more freedom to actually enjoy ourselves. You know, enjoy life more than merely surviving. That is why we are still here."

I can feel the change in Jake—he's beginning to allow joy into his world. Looking at the world through grief has had a huge effect on his life, but now he is taking initiative to reframe his story. I am quiet, giving him some space to process his emotions.

Then suddenly, about halfway through the walk, the sky darkens. Fat raindrops begin to fall, and a rumble of thunder can be heard in the distance. The forecast hadn't said anything about an afternoon thunderstorm, yet that seems to be exactly what's in store.

I look at Jake. "What do you want to do? We can take that shortcut back to the cars or we can find shelter. The only thing I'm not comfortable with is standing in the open."

Without hesitation, Jake opts for the shortcut. We break into a little jog as the rain begins coming down harder, arriving at the trailhead with a loud clap of thunder overhead; we actually see a lightning bolt break across the sky. Without a backward glance, Jake dives into his car. I'm right behind him, jumping into mine.

I call his cell phone: "Whoa! Are you okay?"

"Yeah. Just wet," he laughs. "I'll see you next week."

On the way home, I can't help thinking about how Jake might have felt, having his time and his story cut short. Then again, I remember, there will always be more for him to share. Grief doesn't go away just because the clock ticks or the storm begins or we run out of things to say. As I continue driving home, I realize that *I'm* the one feeling that our early, unplanned ending was unfair. Then I realize something else: This is the feeling that Jake walks around with every single day. His marriage was cut short; his life is constantly upended by things that are out of his control. This new window of empathy is significant, and I know it will be useful in our work together.

• • • • •

The weather isn't only a metaphor for our emotions. Sometimes it can be a trigger, as well. One early spring, while walking with a client who was facing her grief after losing her mother more than 15 years ago, I noticed tiny pink cherry blossoms emerging on the trees. I asked her if she noticed the buds on the tree, and she said yes, very sadly. "What is that like for you?" I asked. She replied, "It is really tough because spring is when my mom died, and I completely remember the cherry blossoms that year. Seeing them just brings me back to that time." So, just as I was thinking about how the little pink blossoms make me happy, and hopeful for warmer weather, this woman was saddened by them.

Just considering all these factors—from drafting a new informed consent to preparing yourself and your clients for changing conditions—might bring up anxiety, frustration, or other emotions for you. The best thing you can do is follow your own advice as a therapist and move through each issue. You know better than to avoid the things that bring up uncomfortable feelings—instead, you can feel the feelings and face the music.

WEATHERING THE MOODS

Sometimes it isn't only the circumstances that present a challenge to the therapeutic frame. It can be very difficult to hold this frame when clients show up annoyed, angry, agitated, ill, or even intoxicated. The key is allowing for flexibility as needed while also being careful not to escalate a client who is already agitated. Consider the following example from a session I had with Joanie.

• • • • •

I can always tell how Joanie's doing as soon as she hops out of her car. Today, she looks keyed up, and as soon as we start walking, she starts in.

"I'm so annoyed with my mom. All I wanted was to talk to her about this family trip, and she just kept changing the subject." Joanie reaches into her pocket, pulls out a cigarette, and half looks over at me. "Mind if I smoke?"

Before I have a chance to answer (was it even a question?), she's lighting up. My first thought is *Wow—I had no idea she smokes!* My next thought is about how safe this *isn't*, given that we're standing surrounded by dry trees and underbrush on this warm spring day. I can almost hear Smokey the Bear admonishing us, "Only you can prevent forest fires."

Joanie admits that she's never told me how she sometimes smokes when she gets mad. "It's pretty infrequent," she adds quickly.

I respond, "Okay, well, I am learning something new about you. Is it safe to say that you must be pretty mad today? How about we sit on that bench for a few minutes, and when you're done with the cigarette, we can go do our usual walk through the woods?"

She agrees, and I breathe a sigh of relief that we won't be setting any trees ablaze today.

After her cigarette, we discuss what the smoking does for her: It lets her relax, helps her blow off steam, and so on. We head off at a brisk pace as she unpacks the story of why she's so mad at Mom today. When we near the end of the trail, I ask, "What was it like for you to decompress with the cigarette, then have the physical exertion of our walk?"

Now much calmer, Joanie laughs a little. "I know smoking is bad for me, but it's only once in a while. I just reach for it when I'm mad. It's kind of automatic. Truthfully, I feel much better having walked off the anger. I will definitely try that before the cigarette next time."

· · · · ·

Sometimes, being outdoors can make it easier to handle a situation like this than if it happened in an office. Other times, being outdoors makes it trickier, especially if a client has a mental health crisis while you're walking outside. Is it really safe to do outdoor walking therapy with someone who has a history of unstable behavior or even self-harming or suicidal thoughts?

The answer has many layers. As I mentioned earlier, my first line of defense in this type of situation happens during my intake call—I do a thorough psychosocial assessment prior to taking any high-risk clients, asking specifically whether they're seeing a psychiatrist, taking medication for any mental health issues, or have had any high-risk events or hospitalizations in their recent history. In the rare case that I feel the situation is too sensitive, I tell the client that walk and talk isn't the best option for them at this time. Most of the time, though, I'll offer to do a few exploratory sessions with the client to see how things go. For these first few walks, we meet in an open area with easy access to the road in case of emergency. This also allows me to learn more about the client's mindset and personality through their physical cues, helping me further assess if we're the right fit for each other.

Occasionally, I've had misgivings during one of these initial sessions. I can remember the sinking feeling of *Yikes—maybe this wasn't a good idea* after walk and talk with a particularly angry person who grew increasingly agitated the farther we got. In moments where you sense that the situation could become unsafe, the same rule applies outdoors as in the office: Trust your gut. Being outdoors can actually offer you more options for helping the client regulate their emotions; you can offer some guidance for working out the feelings through movement (like we saw with Jake in the story in chapter 5), take a pause for some mindfulness work or just to breathe and process, turn around and head back to the trailhead or parking lot, or even take a detour into a more crowded area. In the instance with the particularly angry client, my instinct was to burn off some of their growing emotional energy—I kept us moving and increased our pace, and sure enough, his agitation eventually subsided.

It's also possible that a client will experience a panic attack during a session. Tammie Rosenbloom offered an example of how to handle this scenario. Toward the end of a walk and talk session, her client began dissociating and walked off the path. Despite her fear that the client might go out into the lake, Tammie stayed calm and present. "I asked the client if I could hold his arm," she shared. "He agreed, and I gently guided him back to the path. We then practiced grounding exercises, such as paced breathing and feeling his feet touch the ground with each footstep" (personal communication, May 9, 2022). (Smart choices, since these exercises had the added benefit of helping the client stay on the path.) As they made their way back to the parking lot, they kept a slow, steady pace until the client's panic decreased. Once they reached the cars, Tammie made sure the client was safe to drive and asked him to check in with her once he made it home.

While it's good to be prepared for extreme what-if situations, it's also worth mentioning that I've personally never had an experience this severe with a walk and talk client. However, I have had experiences where clients become extremely emotional while walking. In these instances, I focus all my efforts on their safety and privacy. I try to find a place to rest with them so that they can be present with their feelings; some people want to continue walking, but others appreciate the pause. When they are ready to continue, I find that the walking helps them shake off some of the post-emotion tremors. (It goes without saying that it's a good idea to keep tissues handy.)

Bottom line, it's not easier or harder to maintain the therapeutic frame in walk and talk—it's just different! We therapists love our four walls—there's a feeling of safety that comes from having a physical "container" for our emotional expression. But you can have that same feeling without actual walls. It just takes being strong in your values, being consistent in how you're setting up the therapeutic frame, and finding your own safe, comforting connection within a natural setting.

Chapter 10

Consistency, Care, and Calm

I promised you a day in the life of my walk and talk practice. Now that we have the principles laid out, let's get this show started! Along with giving you a detailed look into how I navigate a variety of client sessions within the ever-changing conditions of the great outdoors, this chapter will also highlight specific ways that the therapeutic frame comes into play.

• • • • •

My trusty clock radio clicks on—it's thirty-six years old and still going strong! I wake up to the glow of the sun behind the trees and an upbeat reggae tune, ready to begin my day with time on the yoga mat. I've come to depend on a twenty-minute flow practice and some deep stretching to take care of the muscles, tendons, and joints that keep me upright and mobile all day long. I also appreciate the quiet introspective time that invites me to reconnect with my purpose as a therapist. As I stretch, I ask myself, "What is my intention today?" Today, I note that I'd like to remain calm, especially under pressure.

Moving on, I make my way to the closet. Deciding what to wear always feels like a light research project, guided by two main questions: What's the weather like today, and who am I seeing? Checking my calendar, I see that I have four clients on my schedule: two paved path walkers, one hiker, and one prone to going off trail and wading through creeks. Consulting my weather app, I see that the day is starting at a sunny forty-five degrees but will warm up to about sixty-five; there's also a 70 percent chance of afternoon rain. All this information translates to the following: leggings, T-shirt, light sweater, medium-weight jacket, baseball cap, and sneakers. I'll bring along my raincoat just in case, but since I don't think it's going to rain hard enough to require the heavy-duty rain boots, I take the chance on leaving those home for the day. One final nonnegotiable is a tube of sunscreen in my bag. After a melanoma scare a few years back, I don't mess around—regardless of the weather or the season, I wear sunscreen on my face 365 days per year.

I arrive at the park at 7:55 a.m., five minutes before my first client is scheduled to arrive. Barring any unforeseen circumstances, I always try to arrive early. This gives me a chance to get settled into "work." I can take a few deep breaths, remind myself why I'm here, and begin to think about the client. Arriving before my client is part of my therapeutic frame, as it sends a message that I am ready, available, and eager to begin the work.

This park is one of my favorites—only a seven-minute drive from my house, it provides a varied landscape with both paved paths and dirt trails through the woods. Just as I finish stuffing my jacket pockets with my keys, phone, tissues, and a tiny water bottle, Joanie arrives with her friendly black Labrador retriever, Pepper, whom she adopted last month. I greet them with a smile; Joanie, however, looks frantic.

"I'm so sorry I'm late," she gasps. "First, I couldn't find my keys, then I couldn't find the leash. I finally found everything and ran out the door!"

Knowing how much anxiety Joanie carries around, holding true to my "yoga mat" intention of staying calm enables me to meet her needs within the therapeutic frame that she consistently expects. I wait patiently as she gets those agitated feelings out while adjusting her jacket, grabbing her hat, and leashing Pepper, then lead us all to our usual trail. Beginning the walk as soon as we meet often helps clients shake off any jitters, enabling us to jump right into the work. The consistency of beginning this way allows clients to be able to feel familiar with the predictability of the session. Once we're on the trail, I follow up on Joanie's comment about rushing out the door: "I hear that you felt really rushed. How was that for you?"

She responds, "Totally anxiety producing. I love having Pepper with me, but there is definitely extra responsibility now that I'm caring for this living thing!"

"Do you want to talk a minute about the anxious thoughts around this?"

"Yes." She reflects for a moment. "I think at this point I might be catastrophizing. I mean, Pepper is not going to die if I leave him at home once in a while. Or if I walk him four times a day instead of six." She laughs a little. I see a sense of relief as her arms swing and her shoulders relax.

Since Joanie and I tend to spend a lot of our sessions talking about her anxious thoughts, I shared a list of cognitive distortions with her a few weeks ago. She acknowledged that becoming familiar with these automatic thinking habits has helped her understand herself better; in fact, she keeps the list handy on her phone for reference when she feels anxious. Since then, we frequently refer to cognitive distortions and other CBT language during therapy; normalizing this language can go a long way toward helping clients be less reactive.

I say to Joanie, "You've really practiced recognizing your automatic thoughts and reframing them to help yourself feel better."

Pepper sniffs at a clump of dandelions, and as he comes to a halt, so do we. We listen to the sounds of the birds singing their spring melody. Joanie takes a deep breath and, unprompted, reflects on what she sees around her. "I'm so happy it's spring! I love that it's getting warmer, the birds are out, and the little flowers in the forest are here." She continues, "I want to start getting out and doing things. I'm just really nervous about meeting people and doing things in real life."

Since Joanie's anxieties often end up focused on social situations, I ask her to tell me one goal she has for herself socially. Joanie doesn't hesitate with her answer: "I want to be able to date. I want to meet someone and just feel comfortable talking with them."

"Help me understand why this is so important to you," I encourage her. "What is the meaning behind this intention?"

She smiles nervously. "I feel like I'm finally getting to be an adult, and I think I need to try to connect with others a little bit more. But it's really hard to meet people. There's only one gay hangout place in town, and I just don't really like going there—it's nerve-racking. I can try online dating apps, but I get nervous about talking to strangers, and I keep thinking about all the things that could go wrong. I just don't want to get hurt."

She's walking pretty fast now, taking the lead on the well-worn dirt trail as she fluctuates from what makes her anxious to what she's excited about. "There's this one person that I've chatted with through Pinterest about our dogs." Noticing that her steps after this confession get playful—she skips a little, and hops on and off a large flat rock in the middle of the trail—offers me clues about the complexity of what she's feeling, poised between her habitual self-protection and her willingness to be vulnerable. A downed log across the path provides the perfect opportunity to convey my care and insight, and I suggest that we pause a minute to absorb what she has been saying. We sit side by side on the log, Pepper panting at Joanie's feet.

"It's so interesting that we are sitting on this log," I say. "I know it probably fell by accident, but right now it's giving us a pretty comfortable place to rest. While the tree used to stand upright, it's now in a different position. Sometimes when things change, there can actually be advantages. You're in a different position now too. I hear that you are feeling like getting to know a new person is a very vulnerable thing. You sound like it would feel safer to protect yourself by not getting involved."

Joanie nods and, after sitting with that reflection for a minute, leans down to pet Pepper as she says, "Thank you for saying that. I think I feel safe here, and I can hear that. It's hard, but I know it's true. The vulnerable stuff is also the stuff that's keeping me from moving forward." As we head back the way we came, she continues, "I look at Pepper and I'm so glad we have each other. I feel like Pep has taught me to be open to at least the idea of new relationships."

Joanie's open-minded attitude creates a ripe space for growth and resilience. We continue our discussion and end with a list of ideas that she wants to try . . . including reaching out to her new Pinterest interest!

It's now 8:50 a.m., and after I've said goodbye to Joanie, I must find a bathroom. Luckily, the park has reopened the bathrooms after a winter hiatus. Literally relieved, I jog back to my car and grab a big drink of water. I have just enough time to check my phone for any notifications of schedule changes before I take a few minutes to prepare for what my next session might bring.

● ● ● ● ●

At 9:15 a.m., I'm on the lookout for Jake. Seeing Jake early in the day is great for me. We always walk fast, and as a morning person, I admittedly have more energy before noon. I stand outside my car and mentally prepare myself, thinking about all that Jake has been dealing with, for himself as well as for his kids. While the term "holding space" applies to every client, I feel that this is the best service I can offer him. Grief work is all about being consistently present, not being afraid to go to hard places, and allowing clients to fully feel their emotions.

Jake pulls up and gets out of his car, ready to move. I greet every client differently depending on their needs that day, but with Jake, we follow the same routine in every session. Same greetings, same trail, same milestones along the way where we stop and observe nature, week after week. For clients who have dealt with the dark side of life's unpredictability, there is comfort, safety, and even freedom in knowing what to expect.

Today Jake begins the conversation: "My son has been waking up in the middle of the night screaming for his mom."

He looks sad, and I think he might cry. I feel like I might, too, and quickly jostle myself back to therapist mode, focused on holding space for the client's emotions.

Jake goes on, "I try to comfort him. You know, just hold him or tell him that I know it's so hard."

"It must be very hard for both of you," I say, validating his feelings before asking him to explore them a bit more. "What was that like for you?"

I can see that he is reluctant to open up, and no wonder. For a strong, silent type like Jake, noticing all these emotions is a bit like learning a new language.

At length, he responds, "I'm not sure. I just wish I could do something."

We continue along briskly, but I'm beginning to think it would be a good idea to slow down so that he can notice more. As our path approaches a stream through the woods, I say, "Jake, let's keep walking, but also try to notice what's happening in the stream. I just want you to feel present."

We watch the water rush over the rocks, listen to the birds calling, feel the alternating warmth and coolness of the sun as the clouds roll by. Reaching back into my morning wishes, I feel a sense of calm, and engage that feeling by asking Jake what he notices.

"I see the water, the green buds of early spring," he says slowly. "I see those two young cardinals flying together." He draws a breath. "I see that time is moving forward. I am here and she is not. I miss her and that makes me feel really sad."

I give him some time, holding the space, acknowledging his pain. Then Jake says something that surprises me.

"See that little waterfall over there?" He points downstream. "That is what keeps me going. The power and energy that comes from the flow of water. If it's in the water, it must live in me too. I have to kind of go with the flow, even when it's hard."

Wow. I'm speechless at his deep insight. In a powerful parallel to the unrelenting flow of water, he, too, must continue to live life while he grieves. But his insight reminds me of another natural symbol I learned about recently, one that is beautifully relevant at this moment.

"Do you know that some people believe that cardinals are your loved ones visiting you?" I ask. "Also, some indigenous people see the cardinal as a symbol of bravery. Maybe those birds are letting you know that you can do these hard things, like grieving the loss of your wife while comforting your son."

He nods and lets out a little shudder of an exhale.

As we continue our session, Jake discusses various situations he's experienced over the past week. I see that he's practicing the language of emotions—my role in this process is merely to acknowledge and validate. We end the session as we always do: a deep exhale from Jake, a nod and smile, and a quick, "See ya next time," before he gets in his car and drives off.

I take a minute in the parking lot after he's gone, thinking about the hesitancy Jake had when he started therapy and how, in spite of it, he has shown up every single week. He has learned to talk about very difficult emotions, feel them fully, and address them. Like a foundation supports a building, the therapeutic frame holds the space that is then filled with deeper parts of the self. Being a stable force in his life has been an important part of his grief work.

I take a deep, cleansing breath—it's always tough listening to these stories. Thinking once again of the intention I set this morning, I remind myself of being present and calm while also taking care of myself. As a therapist, I know that boundaries (including ending sessions on time) are for everyone's good.

Speaking of which . . .

A BRIEF WORD ABOUT BOUNDARIES

This work takes a toll on our physical and mental energy in many different ways. For me, shifting from the office setting to walk and talk has helped me get in touch with best practices for my own well-being. Learning to notice when my legs get tired has made me better at noticing when my mind gets tired. I am mindful to eat a healthy lunch with enough calories to carry me through the afternoon. I also try to drink plenty of water while I'm home and avoid caffeine in the afternoon. (Walk and talk has made me keenly aware of how many bathroom stops I need during the day.) I'm more committed than ever to getting a good night's sleep so that I have more than sufficient energy to show up to a session alert and happy to be there.

I manage my schedule with the same care. As a walk and talk therapist, I do not see clients back-to-back. I don't care if I'm not able to fit in ten clients a day and thus can't make as much money; I have decided that a balance between my work and my own personal needs is more important than a slightly greater financial return. If this is not an affordable option for you, then I encourage you to get creative. Maybe start with just one walk and talk day each week, or perhaps two half days of walk and talk, then gradually work your way up to more.

I also make it a point to avoid long days or working into evening hours. Don't get me wrong, there is still plenty of work to do between sessions or into the evening. (Sadly, freeing my practice from the office doesn't mean I'm free of paperwork.) However, I've learned that spending time alone and with my family at the end of the day is essential to help me reset so I can show up as a fully functioning therapist for my clients. Having interests and needs outside of work is what keeps us healthy and available for those emotionally difficult therapy sessions. Your work is too important for you to burn yourself out.

· · · · ·

Back to our day in the life! Once I get back to my desk at home, I quickly type my morning case notes into my laptop, check the weather app for tomorrow (clear, sunny, and a dreamy sixty to seventy degrees), then text each of tomorrow's clients to confirm their appointment, including the time and location. I always ask for a return text to confirm—even this is part of my therapeutic frame, as it offers clients consistency and reassurance that we are meeting. It also serves a practical purpose for me. When I began my practice, I was stuck a few times at a park with no client in sight. I realized that the two minutes it takes me each day to confirm by text saves me precious time anxiously waiting.

Next, I set up for an intake phone call with a potential new client at 11:00 a.m. Just as I finish up, I notice my stomach alerting me to lunchtime. Before refueling for my upcoming afternoon sessions, I take a moment to reflect on the theme of the morning (and this chapter as it ends). The principles of consistency, care, and calm are the glue of the therapeutic frame, whether in the office or on the trail. From setting predictable meeting places and times to showing up with a grounded, peaceful mindset, to offering a steady presence in the face of strong emotions, these three C's can turn any setting into a space for healing.

Chapter 11

Benefits for the Outdoor Therapist

Therapy is a time for the client to reflect, with the therapist serving as the mirror. Of course, behind the mirror is the therapist who is a whole person with a past, present, and future. What makes the work so interesting is the connection and interaction between client and therapist. This is what makes it extra important for therapists to look after their own needs, not only in their personal lives but also within the session. It's a job requirement to manage our own physical and mental well-being.

When we as therapists arrive at a session, we want to be on our triple A game: awake, alert, and available to our clients. For most of us, this means strict adherence to healthy habits like getting adequate exercise and a good night's sleep, nurturing relationships with our family and friends, making sure we are fed well and dressed comfortably, and even engaging in our own psychotherapy. But here's a revolutionary thought: What about introducing the idea of self-care for the therapist *during a therapy session*? As it happens, walk and talk makes this unique-sounding idea easy to accomplish.

MOVEMENT

Often, the walk and talk therapist is already a physically active person who chooses to practice this way because they understand the benefits of movement and being outside. For therapists who are not used to exercising, walk and talk offers a great way to incorporate an affordable, convenient, and manageable form of exercise into their daily lives. I have therapist friends who literally sit all day long, five days a week, in the same position. Have you ever heard the phrase "sitting is the new smoking"? Give that a moment to settle in. I picture stiff muscles and neck, back, and hip issues. Never mind the eyesight that takes a toll from one telehealth session after another and electronic documentation. I have had therapists call me and say, "I have a bad back, and my doctor said it's from sitting all day long. The doctor recommended that if I could walk with some clients, my back would feel better." If you can integrate walking into your job, then you have another way to improve your overall health. Additionally, walk and talk can alleviate burnout and daily fatigue, though it's a more active and engaging approach.

I'm often asked by therapists who are walk and talk curious about how many miles I walk, and how often. I understand why they're asking—considering the demands of our job, it might sound particularly daunting to add in a few miles per day on foot. On average, I walk about ten miles over two days each week. It's important to note that I started this practice already in pretty good physical shape from marathon training and worked my way up to this weekly average over time. As a result, my body is pleasantly tired at the end of a walking therapy day, but not completely beat.

FRESH AIR

Have you ever had that thing happen where you suddenly wonder how long you've been half-dozing, with open eyes, in your chair while the client was talking? Of course you have—this is a therapist's dirty little secret. You know what I've found that prevents this from happening? Walking! I love getting calls from colleagues who have been trying walk and talk for a few weeks and can't believe how much more alert they feel. Funny how fresh air has that effect!

If you are someone who sees mostly the insides of places (your home, your office, other people's minds), getting outside could be the refresh you didn't know you needed. The benefits of fresh air include improved lung capacity and oxygen flow, a sharper mind, enhanced immune system functioning, and greater energy. By meeting your own needs for fresh air and movement, you are actually doing a better job as a therapist.

CREATIVITY

As therapists, we constantly listen for clues that reflect a client's underlying meaning. We build connections between their ideas and the emotions they are aware of. We tune in to the silences. All of this requires a great deal of focus and creativity. And as we've already discussed in chapter 3, there's a proven and very simple way to boost both of these powers: going outside!

My colleague Julie Edwards, a social worker in Ontario, Canada, practices from a rural cottage on the shore of the Ottawa River, which allows her to offer a variety of outdoor-based settings and activities for her sessions. On any given day, Julie might talk with her clients while walking on the nearby Algonquin Trail, standing over a bonfire on the deck, or sitting in her office with its panoramic view of the river and the surrounding woods. "Prior to setting up this rural office," Julie shared, "I conducted sessions in an office in town. Before changing my practice to a nature-based setting, it was challenging to stay inspired and grounded. Having recently gone through some of my own health challenges, I was reminded that nature is the place where I feel most connected to the present moment and where I feel at my best" (personal communication, May 2, 2022).

As I hope I've shown in the stories I've shared thus far, walking outdoors means constantly finding creative prompts in the weather, the scenery, and the little surprises that happen on the trail. One creative opportunity I haven't mentioned yet is the way walking changes the dynamic of silence during the therapy session. Most of us can recount plenty of sessions where the conversation fell into a deep lull. Sometimes it's due to confusion, emotion, brain fatigue, or even transference if your client gets into a "you can't make me talk!" mood. These occasions are a supreme example of awkward silence, and many of us will go to ridiculous lengths to avoid them. A skilled therapist might embrace these moments and use them as grist for the mill. Still, as my prior supervisor used to say, "If you have to do cartwheels and the client is just watching you, then they're not involved enough." And one of the great gifts of walk and talk is the way it eases a long, uncomfortable pause. If I find myself working harder on the client's issues than the client is—even after more than twenty years of practice, it *still* happens sometimes—I can step back from the conversation, let myself be distracted by bird calls or the babbling of a nearby brook, and take a few moments to process what is really going on.

And the same goes for the client! So often, these silences are necessary for the client to catch up with their own thoughts; letting them have a moment to listen to the whispering trees is much more beneficial than jumping in to rescue them from the awkward pause. Also, you may be surprised to hear that sometimes therapists talk way too much! Silence is okay, even welcome, and sometimes downright powerful, giving space and pause for the digestion of information.

So how big of a difference can this make to your ability to practice therapy? Let's return for a moment to my "day in the life" for a story that shows how the boost from movement, fresh air, and creativity helped me navigate a particularly challenging session.

. . . . .

Taylor and I are faced with a heavy sky for our hike this afternoon. Nevertheless, thinking of the steep climb ahead of us, I opt to leave my umbrella in the car and just wear a hat—who wants to hike with their hands full? Taylor gets out of her car sporting a baseball hat, her bright blue eyes and warm smile radiating under the brim.

"Hi! Nice to see you, Taylor." I pause. "Are you ready to go? Do you want an umbrella? I think it may rain."

"No thanks, I'm fine." She taps her head. "I have my hat, and anyway, I don't care if I get wet. The coaches make us play soccer in the rain all the time!" I'm consistently blown away by Taylor's strong character—she's smart enough to keep learning from the adversity she's faced *and* resilient enough to laugh about it. Getting into her mindset makes me feel like I'm warming up for a race.

"Oh my goodness, I have so much to tell you!" Taylor gushes as we head out on the trail. "This past week has been insane. First of all, we won our first game of the season, and I got to play the whole time! Then we had this party to celebrate. I was having a good time, but then I had this flashback of that night from last summer. I ended up going outside and just sitting down."

"Oh, wow," I respond. "Sounds like a mixed feelings kind of week, but congrats on the game! Also, I'm sorry to hear you had that experience at the party. Do you want to say more about it?"

Up until this point, we've walked side by side, but now the trail has narrowed and we need to walk single file. Taylor steps in front and I follow behind, happy to let her exercise her strength as a natural leader. She plows ahead on the trail, instinctively speaking a little louder but rarely looking back at me. To me, it's a good sign that she has let her guard down and is really talking without any filter.

"I was triggered by a guy who looked like the one who assaulted me. I saw him and I just felt scared and kind of vulnerable. But I felt really good about what I did next! I found my friend and asked her to go outside with me, and right away I felt better. I was so glad that I was with someone who was safe, and she really helped calm me down." She continues, "Oh, and you'd be so proud of me, because you know how I'm always trying to take care of everyone else? Well, I just allowed my friend to take care of me."

"Look at you!" I cheer. "How did that feel?"

"It felt really good." Taylor grins shyly but proudly. "It was hard at first to just talk to her without changing the subject. But you know what? She was really a good listener, and it felt good to talk."

That's when I feel the drops coming down through the canopy of trees. Just a few, though. As we continue walking, it strikes me that Taylor doesn't seem to notice anything. Between her commitment to her therapy and just being a trooper, she keeps trudging up the hill while telling me more about her experience that night. But once we reach the creek, she pauses for a moment and stares down at the water.

At this point, the rain is really coming down. Still, we stand there together. I take a deep breath and she instinctively does the same. Something in her energy lets me know that the lively, empowered spirit she started with has given way to some more complex emotions.

"Taylor, can we take a minute to just notice what's going on for you right now?"

She says, "Yeah. I know it was a lot, and I'm still kind of processing everything that happened last summer." Her eyes are wet, and not from the rain. As I pause and allow the silence to absorb her emotions, I find myself feeling grateful for the unexpected shower. The physical discomfort of being caught in the rain offers even deeper comfort by mirroring Taylor's emotion.

At length, I ask her to name some of the feelings she's having.

"I feel sad that it happened to me. I also feel angry that he got away with it. I'm a little upset with myself, although that has gotten better as I learn self-compassion. I also keep reminding myself that the freeze response served a purpose."

"It's really brave of you to recognize your feelings and to address the issues as they come up in new ways," I tell her.

She reflects for a minute. "I'm actually really proud of myself. I mean, I could be pretending it never happened, and just go on as usual. I think talking about it has helped me find ways to be honest with myself and try to meet my needs when things come up." She takes another deep breath and, through her tears, laughs at herself. "It's pouring, I'm crying, and the creek is gushing. What the heck? I'm one with nature!"

"Yes! How does that feel?" I ask her.

She breathes a deep sigh of relief. "I feel supported. There's something about the connection to all the water. Almost like it's telling me I'm going to be okay, that the pain will wash away." I validate her thoughts as we finish our soggy hike, but it hardly seems necessary now. Resuming her brisk, powerful rhythm seems to have renewed Taylor's strength and sense of agency. It's a beautiful thing to see.

Later that day, as I review my notes, I find myself wondering how this same session might have gone if we'd been in an office setting. Without the movement connecting us, would I have been able to tap into her emotional state so accurately? Without the fresh air and even the rain, would Taylor have found the connections she needed to access her inner wisdom? Would I have been as creative in drawing metaphors that she has now learned to create for herself? Using movement, fresh air, and creativity, I tied the pieces back together. This included helping her own her story, move physically in an empowering way to find her strengths, focus on her support system, and feel connected to the world around her. I smile, thinking about it—at this point, it's hard to imagine doing it any other way. We moved naturally through this process just as decisively as we hiked our famous hill!

AUTHENTICITY

Ever go to therapy in an office where the therapist is sitting nicely in their chair and they just look perfect? Not a hair out of place, no broccoli in their teeth, shiny shoes, neutral-tone clothing. The environment exudes calm control and the comfort of familiarity—it looks just like the last therapist's office you visited. Same tissue box, same clock, same inspiring stock quotes on the wall. ("Feeling is healing"—blergh.)

As the last story showed, walking therapy isn't always neat and pretty. Almost never, in fact. And this isn't just an aesthetic difference. Moving through the outdoors guarantees certain giveaways about the person behind the profession. Our mismatched socks, windblown hair, sweaty faces, and knee braces offer more information than most clients usually glean about their therapist.

Bringing a little extra self to the session is not a bad thing, but it may require engaging in a different kind of conversation or delineating more specific boundaries. Questions from clients can be answered in many different ways. Depending on the person and what they need, we can offer a true but brief answer, use a classic redirect (e.g., "What makes you ask that question?"), or offer a simple affirmative (e.g., "Yes, you are correct in observing X") followed by a quick change of subject.

Still, while I try to maintain an appropriate amount of privacy about my personal life, I sometimes let something more personal slip out. The same shared time, space, and movement that make the clients feel safe with me also makes me feel safe with them. Recently, I was ending a very productive session with a client in the park on a beautiful day. As we took out our phones to schedule our next appointment, I said without thinking, "I won't be available next week because it's a Jewish holiday."

Immediately, I felt that one-of-a-kind cocktail of frustration, embarrassment, and guilt. In a flash, my mind raced through rationales—we'd never discussed my religion, but surely she had assumed I was Jewish, right? Just today she'd spoken of her son attending bar mitzvah parties in a way that seemed to assume I was familiar with that.

The client interrupted my racing thoughts with the innocuous question, "What holiday is it?"

I told her briefly about the holiday. To my surprise, she came back with a joke that clearly demonstrated some familiarity with Jewish culture: "But what food will you be eating?" With our appetites whetted by the hike, we spent a few minutes savoring my descriptions of homemade matzo ball soup and chocolate-covered coconut macaroons, then circled back to how she was learning about Jewish customs and rituals through her son's friends.

Maybe a perfect therapist (though that's not even a thing) would have said, "I'll need to move our regularly scheduled appointment next week due to a conflict" without ever getting into why. Then again, if I'd done that, we might have missed an opportunity to bond over the description of chocolate-covered macaroons, as well as a chance for her to share about her new cultural experiences. Do I regret being a little more open than usual? Not at all. She was curious and positive, and it worked out well for us.

While this personal admission was unintentional, consciously revealing some personal details can be useful within the actual session. My trusted friend and colleague, Jennifer Firestone, is a clinical social worker who practices in Maryland and has over twenty years of experience as a psychotherapist. Based on her training in relational life therapy, which approaches therapeutic work through the lens of helping people build stronger and more meaningful connections, Jennifer has become much more relaxed about self-disclosure. She has seen firsthand how it helps with the client-therapist relationship:

- **We can use our own stories to assist in making a point.** When a client says they feel vulnerable during a time of growth, I may say, "I can relate. Vulnerability was what led me to growth in my practice. How would I have ever started if I didn't face my fears and uncertainties? The alternative would have been quitting."

- **We can use our own stories to help a client feel less alone.** When someone who is going through something opens their soul to you, simply nodding isn't nearly as effective as showing them you understand. You don't always need to include details—saying something like "I've been there" or "I can relate" is often enough to convey your compassion.

- **We can use our own stories to help clients articulate theirs.** Jennifer adds that if you have a personal example that could help the client find words for what they're feeling, consider sharing it. Again, sometimes it is best to omit details, but offering something as simple as "I have had a similar experience, and I know how scary and confusing it can feel" can gently encourage your client to open up more (personal communication, October 7, 2022).

- **We can use our own stories to share positive coping skills.** We therapists have an arsenal of tools and techniques for getting through difficult moments, such as deep breathing, yoga, or a support group. In some situations, offering these solutions in an impersonal manner might come across as cold and clinical, whereas framing them as solutions that have worked for you can be much more impactful. Sometimes, the best solution we can offer is not a solution at all, but simply solidarity. Mental health is about being real.

Bottom line, I like walk and talk precisely because it lets the "dignified professional" mask slip a little. It makes sense, doesn't it? An activity that boosts creativity and reduces stress can't help but loosen us up a little, and sometimes, as "running psychologist" Thaddeus Kostrubala found, that disinhibition can be a good thing.

RELIEVING STRESS

Every person in this world has stress, and therapists are no different. There is no "us" versus "them" since we all carry stress in our lives. Therapists' stress originates in the emotional heavy lifting we do on a daily basis. Combine this with the number of people who need serious help, multiplied by the myriad rules and best practices to keep ahead of, and aggravated on a daily basis by long hours of sitting, institutional pressures and obstacles, systemic problems with the mental health field, and lack of support from insurance, government, or organizations. No wonder therapists need therapy themselves just to avoid burnout!

While walk and talk is not a panacea for our mental health care system or for caregiver fatigue, it does give providers a beacon of hope that it is possible to meet our clients' needs in a healthy, productive manner. Walk and talk has the potential to let providers release some of their stress through movement, fresh air, and nature while also allowing them to do their best work as their authentic selves.

Think for a moment about what it would be like to bring more of *you* into each client's session. Does this sound terrifying? Is it really possible to hold the boundary, the frame, and the space for your client while still being *you*? Take a minute to consider the power of the connection between you and your client, and the biome of safety you have built over weeks or months of care. I promise, being yourself won't mess that up. You must distinguish the forest from the trees. If you allow yourself to lead from a place of caring (not oversharing), you'll find ways to offer your own story in a manner that is helpful and doesn't distract from the work. As Jennifer Firestone said to me, "It's all about being relational. We are spending time with this person as they bare their soul. When they see your authenticity, they feel bonded, supported, and encouraged" (personal communication, October 7, 2022).

Nearly every therapy session presents challenges of one kind or another. We can strain ourselves to prevent those challenges, or we can lean into the moment and trust it—along with our experience, training, and intuition—to guide us.

Chapter 12

Treating Confidentiality with Consideration

In walk and talk therapy, we have a particular responsibility to communicate how we will handle confidentiality. This is important in any therapeutic context, but walk and talk presents an obvious difference. Yes, you can be seen by other people while waiting in your therapist's reception area or even run into people you know as you're on your way to or from their office, but there's no question that therapy in an outdoor public space increases the chance of the client being seen during their session, especially if you live in a small or densely populated community. How can you ensure that what happens at the park, stays at the park?

It's all about being prepared—both you and the client. This means being up front about the possibility of running into someone familiar, starting with the very first phone call. Explaining these circumstances during the initial phone call is also an important opportunity for you to sense whether this will be the best option for the client. (In the case of children and teenagers, I have the confidentiality conversation with a parent or legal guardian during the initial phone screening, then repeat the conversation with the kid once we're together in person.) Just like you, a client may love the idea of walk and talk but still have misgivings about possibly being seen outside with a therapist. If they agree, even enthusiastically, it's important for you to remain alert to their nonverbal cues during the session. Remember, they're looking to you to assess if this is the right format for them. If they seem remotely uncomfortable, discuss it with them later and offer alternatives. Walking therapy has a lot of benefits, but sometimes the benefits don't outweigh the risk of being seen, depending on the client's individual situation.

If you're excited about incorporating walking therapy into your practice, all this risk-oriented communication might feel like a bummer. How are you supposed to build this exciting and potential-packed offering into your practice if you're practically talking clients out of it? Don't stress—in my experience, most clients are comfortable with this particular risk. After all, they often find me *because* they are specifically looking for a walking therapist, which likely means they've considered what an outdoor session would be like. (For those who find you via an internet search, I recommend that you make the details of your walk and talk practice visible to potential clients on your website and business card.)

Even Joanie, despite her struggles with anxiety and social situations, had no qualms about being seen during our time together. During our initial phone consult, after going over the basics (how did you find me, what are you looking for support with, etc.), I launched into my usual spiel:

"Unlike other therapists, I don't have walls to my office. We may see people in the park—I may know someone there, or you may know someone there. It's possible we could even encounter someone we both know. While I can't pretend that we're not there together, I won't tell anyone that we are in therapy. How do you feel about this?"

"Oh, I'm fine with it," said Joanie. "We probably won't see anyone I know. But if I did, I wouldn't care."

"Okay!" I answered. "If you ever do feel uncomfortable, please let me know, as we have other options. Also, I will do my best to make sure that nobody can hear us when we are talking—I'll pause if someone is passing us, or lead us in another direction. I'll also be sending you a form titled 'Informed Consent.' Each line will have a detail about confidentiality. Please take some time to look it over, give it some thought, and let me know if you have any questions."

"Sounds good," Joanie agreed. "I'm sure I'll be fine with it. I'm just really happy to have an opportunity to move a little, especially during therapy."

This is a good example of the typical conversations I have with clients prior to starting walk and talk sessions. Still, I've definitely learned from some mistakes I've made regarding confidentiality. I remember another time, early in my practice, when I got a call from the mother of a teen patient who was neurodivergent. "I think he'll love the walking," said Mom. "My son does not do well with eye contact, so I think he'll really appreciate talking next to you instead of sitting face-to-face." She added that the best place for us to meet would be on a path not far from his school—if we could begin our session right after school was dismissed, it would make the adjustment to their schedule a lot easier. This was early on in my walking practice, and I thought I'd be extra accommodating by making things convenient for her. However, when I showed up to meet with my new patient, many of his peers were walking by on their way home from school. Each time someone passed, he would glance furtively to see if he was being noticed with "this lady." Needless to say, we could barely talk, and I felt bad that I couldn't do anything to protect him. After a few very uncomfortable minutes, I found a side street devoid of people; we ended up walking up and down that street for the duration of our session. Lesson learned: Being overly accommodating is not always the smart thing to do, and if a client (or their parent) seems unaware of the importance of privacy during a session, it falls on me to protect it for them.

The cornerstone of protecting your client's privacy is scheduling a session for a time and place where your session can be as private as possible. But since it's impossible to guarantee that an encounter won't ever happen, I'll share the strategies I've developed for handling challenging issues when it comes to confidentiality.

WHEN YOU'RE RECOGNIZED

What do you do if you see someone you know? It's simple: Smile and keep walking. After all, you are working, and anyone who knows what you do for a living will most likely respect your space. If they don't and begin to talk to you, it's okay to politely say, "Good to see you! Let's catch up another time." No matter who it is—your neighbor, your friend, your mom—in that scenario, your client must come first.

In my experience, these occasions are rare. You'll likely have less trouble with acquaintances interrupting you, and more trouble with keeping your recognition to yourself while your client is talking. This takes a little practice, but it's ultimately not that different from having your phone ring during a session; you simply learn to tune it out.

I remember a session with Jake when, as we rounded the bend of our usual trail, I recognized my friend George walking toward us. I smiled at him, but I did not say hello. For his part, George passed by without giving any sign that he even noticed me. Maybe it was because he knows what I do. Maybe it was his characteristic British subtlety. Maybe it was because of the large headphones he had on that day. Whatever the reason, a glance at Jake proved that my acquaintance with George didn't register with him. We continued our session with no interruption.

WHEN YOUR CLIENT IS RECOGNIZED

Your friends and acquaintances are only one half of the equation. What about a passerby who recognizes your client? Denice Crowe Clark has plenty of experience preparing clients for this possibility. "Even clients who drive in from outside the city occasionally run into someone they know," she writes, "so it is important to address that contingency, no matter the setting" (personal communication, May 10, 2022).

This type of run-in has happened to me, as well. My client, a young woman who had recently moved out of her divorced parent's house, saw an old family friend on our path. They were thrilled to see her and wanted to talk. Fortunately, as Denice advises, I had discussed early on with the client how to navigate this situation if it ever happened. As we'd agreed, she politely answered the friend, then said she needed to get going. The friend smiled, gave her a warm hug goodbye, and that was that. It worked out fine and even provided fodder for our talk, helping her work through feelings of shame around interacting with people from the past as she came to terms with her parents' divorce.

TRIGGERING PEOPLE

If you see a person who might trigger your client, such as an abusive ex-partner, be aware, flexible, and ready to utilize a backup plan just like you would if it started to rain heavily. Again, the priority is safety for yourself and your client. If you need to leave the park abruptly, please look after your client's well-being. Check in with them, ask them what they will do and if they have someone they can call, then follow up later to make sure they are all right.

NOSY NEIGHBORS

What do you do if you run into mutual acquaintances or nosy neighbors? You know, the kind of well-meaning acquaintance who asks questions like "What are you guys doing out here?" or "How do you two know each other?" It's rare that you and your client will be acquainted with the same person or have an encounter with someone you've both crossed paths with in the past. However, when this happens, I recommend offering a friendly but vague answer—"We're just out here taking a walk. Good to see you!"—as you keep moving. Address it with your client once the person has passed to reassure them that their story is safe with you.

PARENTS

One of the most sensitive parts of a therapist's practice is looping in the parents of a child or teenage client. On one hand, our work is to support the child, which means offering a safe container for the thoughts and feelings they confide to us. On the other hand, the parents are entitled to accountability from the therapist they've entrusted with their child's well-being. The weekly session with the child only provides a snapshot of what their life is like; parents are on the front lines of their child's support, and while no parent is perfect (for that matter, no therapist is perfect either), I believe that they genuinely care about what their child is going through and want them to feel good. After all, they're the ones paying for therapy, not to mention driving the child to and from their session.

I have a guiding principle that as long as the child is being driven, then the parents will spend the last few minutes talking with us. I am clear from the beginning that the parents should meet us alone (no siblings or other passengers in the car) at a specific time (usually ten minutes before the official end of the session) at a specific spot in the park that is away from traffic. Alternatively, they can walk to where we are coming from and walk the last ten minutes back with us while we all talk. If possible, I ask the client to lead this debriefing and advocate (with my assistance) for the support they will need from the parents to move forward with their goals for the week. (If I need to have a conversation with parents without the client being present, I will do it separately over a phone or video call.) With guidelines set in place ahead of time, this potentially thorny issue can be surprisingly smooth, as you'll see in the next story.

• • • • •

Shantay has come a long way since we first began meeting three months ago. She has worked through some of her concerns about wanting to know her birth mom and is beginning to understand herself as someone who was born Black and lives with a mixed-race family. Like many teenagers, Shantay still struggles to balance her personal identity with wanting to fit in. But since the all-time low of the bullying incident, she has found ways of increasing her self-esteem, being around positive people like her Girl Scout friends, and strengthening the positive coping skills she's learned, such as exercise and meditation.

Today, however, Shantay's eyes are glued to the ground when her mom drops her off. It's clear to me that something has happened.

"Hey, how's it going?" I greet her. "Are you all right?"

"Not really," she mumbles. "I had a bad weekend, and my mom wants me to talk about it."

"Okay—do *you* want to talk about it?"

"I will." She takes a long pause—I give her all the time she needs, and finally she speaks again. "I was starting to feel like this one kid at school was truly my friend, but then I found out through social media that she was hanging out over the weekend with one of the girls who bullied me. I was scared that she wasn't going to like me anymore. So then I asked that girl if we could hang out, but she said only if we are with the other girls—the bullies. They were all going to the mall on Saturday afternoon. I didn't know what to do."

Shantay takes a deep breath even as she continues walking at a brisk pace. She doesn't seem to notice that she's walking through puddles and getting mud all over her leggings. I can see her entire focus is on getting out her words.

"I ended up lying to my mom," she finally says. "I asked if I could go to the mall with the girl who is nice. My mom took me, but when she picked me up, she saw the whole group, even the bullies. She's warned me so many times to stay away from them." Her fists hit the sides of her legs in frustration. "Ugh. It's so confusing. They never let me do anything! I don't know why they think that I'm going to do something reckless. I can't wait to turn eighteen and go to college. I want to make my own decisions and be independent."

We continue to walk along the wooded path, now talking pretty quietly. A group of runners passes us. We see only their backs, but when I look back at Shantay, her face has changed.

"Oh! Wow!" She breathes in. "I was surprised . . . It looks like a cross country team. I don't think they're from my school—I didn't recognize anyone I know."

I can tell that she's still on edge. "Do you want to walk on that side path we sometimes take? In the interest of your privacy, we might want to do that today." This idea seems to relax her, and we make our way along an offshoot of the trail until we reach a log by the side of the creek.

We sit down and I ask if there's anything else going on for her around this issue of wanting independence. For a moment, Shantay stares blankly at the water flowing around rocks before continuing. She talks about trying to find her birth mom on her own once she turns eighteen. She talks about the complicated thoughts and feelings that come up as she navigates these different aspects of her life and identity. At one point, she jumps onto a nearby rock, throws her arms in the air, and declares, "I am just me. Not them." Her mood seems lighter now, and I can't help but think about how brave she is. She carries a weight that we both see is growing as she gets older and goes through changes; at the same time, her strength is growing too.

About five minutes from the end of our session, I ask Shantay the same question I ask every week: "What do you want to share with Mom today?"

She answers, "I don't really want to tell her all the details, but I am okay with sharing some of the strategies we talked about for identifying my emotions, and how I can journal or listen to music when I feel upset."

Up ahead, we see Mom making her way down the path. I have encouraged her to meet us away from the parking lot so that we have a little more privacy and can talk together for a few minutes as we walk back to the car.

Mom, smiling, says, "Hi. How'd it go today?"

Shantay gives me a side glance, which I interpret as *You start!*

"Good," I respond. "She's been using our time really well. Shantay, do you want to share something?"

"We talked about how when I get upset, I should write things down," Shantay says. "Also, that I'll exercise for ten minutes when I'm angry, before doing anything else."

While I'm happy she's given her mom some concrete results of our time together, I wish that she would let her mom in a little more. But Mom comes through for her daughter with nothing but positive support: "Shantay, I'm really proud of you for working on this. I know it's a lot to push through, and I think you're doing a good job even talking about your feelings. If there's anything I can do to help, let me know."

I am warmed by Mom's sentiments, and I see that Shantay is a little teary-eyed. I ask one more time if Shantay would like to say more about the feelings she processed during session. In almost a whisper, Shantay glances down, kicks a little dirt, and says, "I talked about being confused about the girls at school." And then she flashes her smile and says, "But it's also okay just to be me right now. Not anyone else." I smile and ask if there's more. She scrunches her nose, shakes her head no, and at that point, I realize I have gotten as much out of her as possible. I also know that the second half of our session was about her biological mom, and she has said to me that she doesn't want to share those thoughts with her (adopted) mom. She is very careful not to hurt her. I respect that, and we finish up our conversation. As Shantay is about to get into the car, she gives me a sweet half-smile and a quiet thank-you.

Wow, those little thank-yous go a long way! I sit in my car for a minute reflecting on this session. Later that day, after case notes have been written up and final emails have been answered, I'm still thinking about it. I take a book outside with me—the spring air is refreshing, the dogwoods are flowering, and the sun is setting later each day. But soon I notice that I'm not reading, just sitting in stillness, looking at the sky, thinking about the universe and how small we are. We are all cogs in the wheel, living, breathing, witnessing, supporting, and growing.

WHEN STRANGERS APPROACH

There's a third category of potential interrupters: the well-meaning strangers who stop you and your client to ask for directions, request your help taking a photo, ask for your signature on a petition, or just share their enthusiasm for the beautiful setting. These types of encounters are best met with a simple true-but-not-too-revealing answer such as "Sorry, we're in a meeting right now." (This response can sometimes work for people you actually know, as well.) Often there's nothing people (especially Americans) respect as much as being on the job—use that to your advantage. Bear in mind, though, that if you have more sessions that same day, it's probably a good idea to change your route so that you don't have to repeatedly use the same line with the same eager solicitor or friendly hiker.

WHEN CONFIDENTIALITY CONFLICTS WITH A MENTAL HEALTH CRISIS

Last but not least, the million-dollar what-if question: What if a mental health crisis were to happen during your walk and talk session and was noticed by other people? In that case, your number one priority is looking out for your client's safety. If there is no need to disclose your therapist-client relationship, then do not tell others in the park about that status. However, if you need to call 911 in a crisis, inform the client that in order to keep them safe, you may need to disclose to the first responder that you are their therapist. Let the client know that this will help them navigate the appropriate next steps. Remember that you are allowed to break confidentiality if the client is in imminent danger or is a threat to themselves or others. Please let this ethical standard be your guide as you care for your client.

YES, AND . . . !

Now that we've gone through all these rare and mostly unlikely scenarios, how are you feeling about walk and talk? Inspired? Scared? Unsure? A little bit of everything?

Have you ever heard of the game "Yes, and . . ."? It's a trick they use in improv comedy skits to keep the plot moving forward—no matter how crazy or off-the-grid the action gets, the players find a way to build it into a fresh new story. Walk and talk—like life itself—is one giant game of "Yes, and . . ." We try our best, build our frame, seek out guidance, and use all our tools and insight to more or less make it up as we go along! You never really know what to expect from a session, whether it's inside or outside, but do you quit? I hope not. You have so much to offer as a clinician. The world needs you now, doing your best work with the best tools at your disposal. Now, stop overthinking this and get your shoes on!

Summer:

Cultivating Strategies for a
Thriving Walk and Talk Practice

> **"** *Believe in the integrity and value of the jagged path.* **"**
>
> —Cheryl Strayed

Chapter 13

Walk and Talk with Diverse Populations

When I began my walk and talk practice, I wanted to be as inclusive as possible. Hoping that all would feel welcome in the space I was establishing, I welcomed everyone from children to older adults, individuals to groups, and of course all body types, races, ethnicities, and religions.

While I have been open to all populations, there are plenty that I have yet to work with. In the interest of helping us all learn the best way to serve these folks within the walk and talk context, I reached out to a few trusted colleagues in the walk and talk therapy community for their experience working with diverse populations. I'm very grateful for their generous insight; at the same time, I must note that these stories are specific to each therapist's experiences. Glean what you can, be on guard against generalizing, and use these stories to inform your self-education.

PHYSICAL DISABILITY

Let's start with the obvious: Walk and talk therapy isn't limited (or shouldn't be) by the ability to walk. Between non-disabled and disabled people, there's a wide range of capacities and comfort levels that can and should be accommodated in walking therapy. I spoke about this topic with Ben Spangenberg, the national leadership program director at RespectAbility, a nonprofit that reduces stigma and advances opportunities for people with disabilities. He shared with me that people who are born with a disability are often more shut in their homes, which can make the prospect of outdoor therapy more enticing, but also more difficult. In addition, since it's not uncommon for disabled people to have a lower income, they often depend on their insurance benefits for support in accommodating their lifestyle, which means they typically search for an in-network mental health care provider. Both factors, Spangenberg says, can mean a limit to their options for therapists. (This is important to note for any insurance company representatives reading this right now; see more in chapter 14.)

Here are a few ways for walk and talk therapists to better accommodate individuals with disabilities:

- Consider designing your website with language and imagery that welcomes people with all ranges of bodies and ability levels.

- Offer a sliding scale fee structure not only for people who are disabled, but also for other lower income individuals.

- Seek out an outdoor meeting space that is manageable for a person in a wheelchair. This includes ample handicapped parking, a flat paved walking path, and one that is wide enough to navigate side by side.

Another potential issue in this context can be the therapist's use of language. As therapists, it's our responsibility to use terminology that is most comfortable for the client. In addition to asking the client how they want to be addressed or referenced (some are fine with identifying as "a disabled person" while others prefer "a person with a disability"), it's important to go the extra mile in how you reference your work with them. Case in point: I've heard some clinicians refer to walk and talk therapy with a person in a wheelchair as "roll and talk." When I asked Spangenberg about this, he was clear that this term sounded a little too "cutesy." Following his lead, I continue to use the term "walk and talk therapy" regardless of the client's physical capacity.

Finally, it is imperative that we not burden a client with the task of educating us. Before meeting with a client who has a physical disability, I do some advance research on their particular disability or condition, their possible range of limitations and strengths, and the various facets of being born with that disability versus encountering it later in life. Since the range of physical disabilities is vast, and varies from one individual to another, the main takeaway here is *make no assumptions*. Keep an open mind, prepare yourself as much as you can, and continue assessing and educating yourself as you go.

I was contacted some time back by a patient named Lexi, who identifies as a disabled person and was looking for support after breaking up with her longtime partner. During the phone intake, she shared that she was born with a developmental disability that left her paralyzed from the waist down and required the use of a wheelchair. We discussed what this would mean for our sessions and set up our session in a place that had a flat, wheelchair-accessible path.

I was waiting in the parking lot when Lexi texted me, ten minutes before our session was scheduled to start: "My van is blocked in my parking spot, since someone parked illegally right next to me. I'll be late." Just five minutes later, she texted again: "Problem solved. See you soon." A neighbor had come out to help Lexi move her van to a place where she had room to use the van's wheelchair lift.

Once Lexi arrived, though, we immediately faced another obstacle: The track we were going to walk was quite crowded that day, thanks to the beautiful spring afternoon. I immediately realized I should have planned better for this unique situation, but Lexi was unfazed and suggested we just go around the block a few times.

As I walked and Lexi wheeled herself, arms pumping, I quickly realized that walking with someone in a wheelchair does *not* mean less walking. We covered two and a half miles together; by the end of our session, I was as tired as I've ever been! I shouldn't have been surprised—Lexi kicked off our conversation sharing her passion for wheelchair sports, including basketball and tennis, and the boost in mood and self-esteem that she's always associated with athletics. As she put it, "One thing that helped me succeed in life is exercise."

Another thing I noticed early in our session was the difference in how we looked at each other. In her chair, Lexi was about a foot and a half shorter than me. Rather than ignore this unusual dynamic, I asked her how it felt for her. Lexi said she was used to it; in fact, she was more comfortable with a little extra distance. I was grateful that it didn't cause any problems for her; for my part, it took some extra effort to adjust my awareness to the height difference, as well as to practical concerns like curb cuts, pacing, and any obstacles or stumbling blocks we might encounter. Still, it was a challenge that I greatly enjoyed, not only for the opportunity it gave me to expand my practice but also because working with Lexi proved to be meaningful and enlightening, simply by virtue of the individual she is.

Later, Lexi said how happy she was to have an in-person, outdoor session. As someone who spends most of her day working online, Lexi loved how it felt to reconnect with her body and with nature during therapy, adding, "I felt way more open and creative in my expression since I was moving while we were talking."

EATING DISORDERS

I've received frequent questions from other therapists about doing walk and talk with a patient who has an eating disorder. My initial answer is always the same: I believe that a therapist needs specific training and experience to address these types of issues. For more depth, I looked to Amanda Talley, a therapist and founder of Wildernew® Outdoor Therapy, who specializes in treating clients with issues like eating disorders and compulsive exercise.

Before meeting her clients in her outdoor "office," a 200-acre nature preserve in a suburb north of Dallas, Amanda has a specific screening process that involves talking through their treatment history, current food intake and eating habits, activity levels, and whether they have recently seen a physician or had a full medical workup. She asks if there are any medical concerns (e.g., electrolyte imbalances, low weight, heart rate, bone density) and sometimes, depending on their stage of treatment or recovery, also reaches out to their psychiatrist, doctor, or dietitian to determine whether movement and outdoor therapy are indeed appropriate.

When Amanda meets a client for their first walk and talk session, she begins by discussing their intentions for movement. She asks questions to determine their own awareness of their body and prompts them to talk about some of their challenges regarding movement—all of this will inform the duration and pace of their walk. Sometimes she asks to change the route to make the walk less demanding. Other times, she incorporates breathing exercises or stretches that calm the nervous system, or embodiment activities like sitting for a bit or even eating a snack. Throughout the course of treatment, Amanda emphasizes that it is very important to have regular phone calls with the client's medical support system (psychiatrist and dietitian) to ensure the activity level is appropriately serving the client.

"I think of one client who was struggling to complete snacks," Amanda writes. "We agreed to eat one together during a session. We sat down at a picnic table and checked in at the beginning, middle, and end. While the client is usually eager to move, she found peace in taking a rest, and even opted to sit for the duration of the session. We reflected on how her mind and body often run like she's on a treadmill, creating anxiety and compulsive, mindless behaviors. She acknowledged that the slower pace allowed her to have a very different experience—she was more present, relational, curious, and relaxed. The work we did in that session served as a catalyst to further explore movement, her relationship with her body, and the impact on emotions and eating disorder behaviors" (personal communication, May 13, 2022).

Clearly, there are meaningful ways to incorporate outdoor therapy even with clients for whom exercise can be triggering. With the right insight and expertise, therapists can develop a nuanced version of walk and talk that allows this unique clientele to access the healing powers of movement and nature.

AUTISM SPECTRUM DISORDER

Walk and talk therapy with neurodivergent clients can be amazing. As you can imagine, traditional in-office therapy for people challenged by social interactions can potentially be awkward or uncomfortable. By inviting these clients into a space that feels more relaxed and less stressful, walk and talk offers more opportunities for growth and real-life application. A few things to consider before taking on these clients include their transportation, their level of independence, and how to connect with their family member or caregiver. Consider who will be driving them, who will be paying, and what their relationship is like. Oftentimes the initial call will come from a parent, even if the patient is of adult age, so your screening process will need some adaptation if a legally designated caregiver is calling on behalf of a neurodivergent young adult. If the client is a child, be sure to check in with their other providers and school team. Check specifically to see if the client's current social workers or educational team think this format is safe and favorable.

Aliza Graber, a clinical social worker in Maryland, works with teens and young adults who identify as neurodivergent and has incorporated walk and talk sessions with a number of her clients. Like Amanda in the previous section, Aliza stresses that the first order of business is assessing the client's individual needs and challenges and screening for any major concerns that might come up while they are outdoors. Barring any major issues, the conditions of walk and talk can be uniquely effective for neurodivergent patients. "One of the benefits of walk and talk therapy is that we don't have to sit across from each other and make eye contact," Aliza shared, "which can feel intimidating and overwhelming for those with autism. By walking outside, there is a more casual and natural flow, and we can have moments of silence that don't need to be filled. It also adds a sense of camaraderie and togetherness because we are walking the steps alongside each other on equal footing" (personal communication, May 29, 2022).

The path that Aliza typically uses for her sessions offers some gentle challenges that have proved very useful in her work with these clients. On a nice day, they often have to contend with hikers and bikers coming from both directions, offering practice in handling the unexpected. If there's been a storm recently, they have to sidestep mud puddles or fallen tree branches, which helps to develop frustration tolerance. "One time we even stumbled upon a lost dog," Aliza recalled, "which was a great opportunity to work on some problem-solving skills as well as managing uncomfortable feelings!" (personal communication, May 29, 2022).

There are specific challenges in working with these clients, such as helping them be open to trying a different strategy or changing their route. Even with all her training and experience, Aliza always spends some time thinking about what might work best for that patient on that day before her session begins. Moreover, given the diversity amongst specific diagnoses, Aliza often works with the client's parents or caregivers to assess their individual needs. Still, these challenges are well worth the extra effort they require. "I have had a few powerful moments along the walking path," Aliza remembers. "For the client who came upon the lost dog, we worked together to find the number to call and make a report. The client had a lot of sad and worried feelings come up, and we used this opportunity to explore those feelings and how to cope with them. With another client, a teen, we stopped at a playground—they really enjoyed playing on the jungle gym and the swings. That element of play and freedom allowed them to open up more about some of their challenging feelings" (personal communication, May 29, 2022).

CHILDREN UNDER AGE SEVEN

As every parent knows, there's one cardinal rule for spending time outdoors with young children: Be prepared for just about anything. The same rule holds true for walk and talk therapy with younger kids. Expect the walk to be a lot shorter (in terms of distance) and more exploratory. Children want to take their time investigating details in nature—I have seen children who want to squat and stare at a flower for a good ten minutes or pick up rocks on the creek bank for the entire session. Children may go off the trail without asking, insist on wading through the creek to find a fish, or sit on a log and throw sticks in the water. As much as possible and within the bounds of safety, give yourself permission to slow down, take your time, and use these exploratory moments as an opportunity to get to know your client. You may be surprised how much a child will share when their energy is occupied this way.

Vanessa Robin, another Maryland-based clinical social worker, shared an example from her work with a six-year-old boy who had experienced significant trauma in the first two years of his life and was starting to display aggressive behavior.

"Prior to the session, I had to make sure I was competent in terms of play therapy for six-year-olds," Vanessa recalled. "We met in a park where we could walk through the woods, and typically spent about half the session doing various methods of play therapy and the other half of the session walking and talking. We often walked down to the creek so that we could use the sounds and flow of the water for mindfulness practice, and so that the client could throw rocks into the creek—each rock represented some aspect of anger or pain that he wanted to release" (personal communication, May 25, 2022).

Like Vanessa, practitioners working outdoors with children may still include some of their office-based play therapy tools, such as books or figurines, during a walk and talk session. When I meet with a young child, I will often bring a tote bag with paper, markers, and some glue for nature-based art projects. Vanessa also mentioned that at one point, she and the client stopped during their walk to read and discuss the book *Owl Babies* (Waddell, 1992), which proved to be a turning point in the client being able to talk about his feelings regarding his non-custodial parent. Throughout the relationship, Vanessa also spent a lot of time consulting with the client's parent to make sure that the client had time and space at home to practice the skills they were working on. (She says the client was often part of these conversations, though not always.)

REFUGEES

The past decade has brought a renewed understanding and urgency for serving the mental health needs of refugees, asylum seekers, and immigrants. Movement in the outdoors can be especially therapeutic for these clients. I've found that being in an open space with familiar natural features, such as a wooded trail or creekside path, can feel a lot more like home than an office space surrounded by material items that may seem excessive and so very American. Further, movement can help these clients connect with their bodies, increase their sense of agency, and process trauma in an embodied way.

Each new client offers us a fresh opportunity to educate ourselves as therapists, and perhaps none more so than a client who has newly immigrated to your country. As the world's challenges multiply, it's incredibly important to hold a higher level of consciousness for the issues that surround these groups. What does it mean to arrive in this country fleeing oppression, war, or indigence? What communication barriers will they face, and how will language impact their adjustment? What does it mean to arrive in a land that appears to be plentiful and yet, there is a deficit in one's own needs being met? These are only a few considerations for the therapist who works with this population, and the responses can vary widely. Therefore, when meeting with a newly settled client, one of the first things I do is ask about any pertinent terminology they would like me to use—from their ethnic identity, to how they'd like to be addressed, to any customs or manners that help make them comfortable in our relationship. This is a good rule of thumb with any client, as words are a foundational way of validating and affirming each client's experience.

Some time back, I was referred by a fellow social worker to Ruby, a thirty-year-old Black woman newly immigrated to the U.S. In referring her, the social worker mentioned that she felt Ruby would be a good candidate for walk and talk. On our phone consultation, Ruby was very quiet and guarded, but opened up quite a bit when we met for our first session. She told me how she managed to save money and advocate for herself and her daughter in order to escape an imminently dangerous situation. As I listened to the stories of all that Ruby had endured, my first priority became clear.

"I want you to feel safe with me and trust me with your story," I told Ruby as we walked. "I will do my best to learn about your home country's political structure and religious practices, but please bear with me if I ask some questions about your particular experience." She nodded, seeming to appreciate my willingness to research so that she was not burdened with having to explain everything to me. Later on, she expressed that addressing our differences early on was a relief. It was as if I had cleared the air before it became an issue. We talked about how even though we look different and have lived different lives, she is the expert on herself, and we were there to focus on her needs.

In addition, while the social worker had already greenlit Ruby as a good candidate for walking therapy, I asked Ruby after that first session if she felt comfortable with it *and* if she wanted to do it again. That day, and over the weeks that followed, Ruby expressed her appreciation for the freedom to talk while being surrounded by the tall trees. She talked about how nature played a type of survival role in the past—her happiest memories of childhood were in the woods or in streams with her cousins. In addition, being often alone on the trail provided the kind of privacy Ruby needed to open up in therapy.

There will often be special practical considerations for walk and talk with these clients. Since Ruby lived in a different part of town from where I typically practice, I met with her at a suburban park within walking distance of her home. We had to be extra clear in our communication about timing so that we were always back in time for her to meet her child when the school bus dropped her off. As the weather grew colder, I coordinated with the resettlement agency to ensure that Ruby had a pair of boots and a winter coat that would let her continue our walks comfortably.

As the therapy continued into the winter, Ruby and I developed a genuine connection. We worked together for over a year, and as she became more settled in her new life, our sessions became less frequent. It was encouraging to see therapy take its natural course, as Ruby learned skills for protecting her own mental well-being.

EVERY SESSION IS AN OPPORTUNITY

It goes without saying that this list is limited. There's no way to cover every distinct population we might encounter. Each new client we meet offers a renewed reminder not to make assumptions. No matter how a person may present, we must never assume that they feel just as comfortable about walking (and talking) in public as we may feel. Each session is a fresh opportunity to have a conversation about how we show up, what it feels like, and how we can figure this out together.

Chapter 14

Common Questions About Walk and Talk Therapy

Considering the volume of questions I am asked by fellow therapists, I couldn't close the cover on this book without addressing as many of them as I could. Along with combing through my inbox for the "outlier" questions that I haven't covered in the previous chapters, I surveyed curious therapists to find out the top questions they had about walk and talk therapy. As usual, I've included words of wisdom from other experienced walk and talk therapists alongside my own observations.

It goes without saying that no book can cover every single contingency for every type of practice or client. I've done my best to collect the most common questions I've been asked, but the real goal of this chapter is to help inform your own thinking about what you might encounter in your specific walk and talk practice. That said, if you have a burning question that hasn't been addressed by the end of this chapter, don't be left hanging—the "Walking, Outdoor Therapists" Facebook group offers a friendly platform to explore unanswered questions!

COMMON QUESTIONS

DO YOU ALLOW PEOPLE TO BRING THEIR DOGS TO A WALK AND TALK SESSION?

One of the things that I love about meeting my clients outside is that I learn more about them than I would in a confined office setting. It's one thing for a client to tell you about their experiences, but when you witness their interaction with the world around them, you often learn so much more!

This was highlighted for me by a client who brought his dog every week to our session. When I would ask him questions about his feelings, he would direct these questions to the dog, then he would tell me how the dog felt. Projecting? Yes indeed—and it worked! This beloved dog was a conduit for the client's emotional state, enabling a young man who had not been raised with the language of emotions to talk about his feelings.

Ideally, a client would first ask if they can bring their dog, but not all clients think ahead like that. If they do ask in advance, feel free to ask the client any questions that would be important to you. (A few that come to mind for me include "Is he friendly?" "Will you be able to keep him on a leash?" and "How will he do when he passes other dogs?") Emphasize the point that the therapy comes first, and if they can safely include their dog, it's fine to bring their furry friend along. If you're unable to "screen" the dog ahead of time, try it for one session, see how it goes, and have a follow-up conversation about it with the client. Bottom line, if the dog proves to be distracting from the therapy, then you probably want to think twice about including it.

WHAT IF YOU GET LOST?

This entire book is focused on how to set up a successful walk and talk therapy session. We learn, we understand, we try things, and we learn some more. Still, we need to be mindful that heading out into the wild with a client means taking on additional responsibilities. You are not only making a commitment to mental healing; you are also providing as much safety and security in your sessions as possible. In the great outdoor office space, this starts with considering what is in your control and what isn't. Things you can control include:

- **Planning to walk in parks or paths that are safe.** I feel most comfortable following well-marked trails or paved paths. I also prefer to keep to areas where cell service is available. If you are based in a more rural area that has spotty service, create a solid safety plan in case of an emergency. Use common sense—avoid trails that hug cliffs, have narrow overpasses, or require greater athletic ability or training. (Remember, this isn't personal training—this is therapy.)

- **Following general hiking or walking etiquette.** When a client heads off the trail for whatever reason (usually to explore), I am mindful that we aren't ruining special plants and are never going so far that we lose sight of the blue blazes.

- **Keeping an eye on environmental and weather-related concerns.** We've covered this in detail, but it bears repeating.

- **Keeping a cool head and using common sense.** Even after all I've learned from the past decade of walk and talk, the following story reminds me that in this practice, you always need to manage your expectations and be able to go with the flow.

• • • • •

Taylor has just graduated from college and, in the fall, plans to travel with the Peace Corps to Africa, where she will spend the next two years improving local women's health facilities and coaching girls in after-school sports. When I ask how she feels about going away, she answers, "Nervous, excited, scared, and determined." Sounds about right to me!

The night before our usual session, she texts to ask if we can meet at a different part of the trail that is within walking distance of her home. She'd suffered a minor car accident that left her unhurt but also without wheels for the time being.

I pull up to the place she suggested and see Taylor sitting on the edge of the curb. After asking about how she's feeling physically, I ask if she's hiked this section of the trail before.

"No," she admits, "but I know there's an entrance here. I've seen people go in and out."

Sure enough, we find a clearing in the brush—likely an improvised entrance that some neighbors made to get to the main trail. We begin walking on a path that has clearly been well traveled, though there are no blue blazes nearby. Already, my awareness level is turned up a notch; I begin taking note of landmarks around us as we delve into the forest.

Taylor starts by talking about her plans for Africa but quickly moves into the anxiety she's feeling about going to a new country. "I can't believe that I'm going. I mean, everything will be so different. The language, the signs, getting around. I mean, even just going out. How will I know where to go?"

I reflect back, "Sounds like you have been thinking about this. How does that feel to you to go into the unknown?"

Taylor says, "I mean, it's scary. Definitely. But also exciting and adventurous!"

At that moment, our walk is stopped by a fallen log across the path. I look around and realize we've come a good distance without any trail markers to guide us.

"Taylor, do you know where we are?"

She responds, "Um. No. Do you?"

Realizing that we might be a tad lost, I try to look brave, or at least like I've got this. Since I'm confident that there is at least one easy solution—doubling back and exiting exactly how we entered—I decide to use this as a therapeutic here-and-now moment.

"Let's take a minute to acknowledge that we may have lost the trail," I say as I take a deep breath. "I know this isn't ideal, but maybe we can appreciate the irony of this considering that you were just talking about going into the unknown!"

Taylor laughs a little. "I know. I guess we'd better figure out what to do because this is definitely going to be easier than when I get lost in Africa!"

I nod in agreement, while also noticing a blue trail blaze about fifty yards away, and just beyond it, a clearing that I now recognize as a section of the main path. Keeping this to myself for now to give Taylor an opportunity for empowerment over her own problem-solving, I respond, "And yet, you will be prepared to stay calm and think through your options." I'm affirming her future while also trying to bring us guidance in the present. "What are our options and our resources right now?"

Taylor lists some ideas as though she prepared them ahead of time. "We can look for the blue blazes on the trees. We can try to use the GPS on our phones. We can turn around and go back where we came from. We can see if there's a way to get around our obstacles and try to make our own path until we see the big path."

I nod in agreement. "You've got this. So many good ideas. What do you want to do?"

Taylor bravely says, "I'd like to keep going into the woods for a few more minutes. I'm hopeful we can find some clues. Do you mind walking through this part with me?"

A minute later, she spots the blue blazes. Soon, we're back on the familiar section of trail that we walked earlier.

I ask her, "Taylor, what was that like for you?"

She's smiling as she says, "It was a little scary being lost. I mean, we could have turned back, but I really didn't want to do that. I was glad I made the decision to keep going. This part of the well-worn trail is so pretty. I love this view from the top and love to look down toward the stream. It was worth the discomfort of moving through the branches."

"Yes. And what about those feelings of being scared, and then relieved? What can you find inside yourself that helped you move through the feelings?"

She sighs, "Yeah. I think I'm ready, and it's okay to have those feelings. I mean, I don't really like being scared, but I can be with it. I don't react or freak out. I just know it's there and then think about what I need to do. In a way, it makes me feel capable of handling big emotions like fear of the unknown. I don't know, I may actually be feeling . . . brave."

I smile at Taylor and reinforce all the good feelings she's having. I know she can do this, but most importantly, *she* knows she can.

HOW DO YOU HANDLE UNEXPECTED ENCOUNTERS WITH ANIMALS?

Great question! I have definitely had my share of animal happenstances, as have most other walk and talk practitioners I know. Some can be very touching and therapeutic, while others can be quite alarming, like the time a squirrel ran out at me and bumped into my leg!

The first thing to note is that, as Denice Crowe Clark pointed out, most clients do not consider the possibility of encountering animals when they sign up for a walk and talk session. As a result, she has learned that even seemingly benign animals (ducks, turtles, squirrels) can be uncomfortable for some clients. "I had one client freak out over birds flying overhead," she recounts. "I learned another was fearful of off-leash dogs which, unfortunately, is a normal occurrence in the park despite leash laws" (personal communication, May 10, 2022).

I encourage walk and talk therapists to study their natural environment before getting started. Make a list of the risks associated with your area, learn more about what to do in certain circumstances, and consider taking a class at a local camping store or nature center to learn how to handle surprise animal encounters. While you don't have to be a wildlife expert, what you cannot do is ignore risks. Please take your role of being in charge seriously and do what you can to take basic precautions for unlikely but possible encounters.

When I hiked in Wyoming, I carried bear spray, as did all the other hikers around me. When I did see a bear, I felt prepared, kept my hand loosely on the spray, and thanked my lucky stars that the bear showed no interest in me. But not all animal encounters are obvious risks, which makes it very important to pay attention to each animal's behavior. Deer are prevalent in my neck of the woods, and a deer encounter is almost always peaceful. However, I was recently walking with a client on a pretty narrow trail when we noticed a young buck about thirty feet ahead of us. His antlers looked injured, but also very pointy! My client and I froze as we watched him carefully; the deer paused and looked right back at us. It was a face-off! Wanting neither to frighten nor challenge him, I suggested to my client that we back away slowly to where we'd just come from. My client, a badge-earning Eagle Scout, was in full agreement. As soon as we gave the deer his space, he ran off into the woods.

Still, as long as the therapist is prepared for these situations, animal encounters can often be used as a valuable tool in the session. Seeing a snake naturally brings up a discussion about anxiety, panic, or managing the fight-or-flight response. When my client and I noticed an owl in the trees overhead, we stopped to consciously indulge our awe and appreciation for the chance to see this amazing creature. Sometimes the encounter is just plain weird, prompting both the client and therapist to understand their environment on a deeper level.

"The strangest animal I encountered," Denice Crowe Clark shared, "was a coyote sunning himself in the middle of the park meadow. It turns out coyotes are quite common in cities and help control the rodent population, but when they make themselves that conspicuous, it can mean they are seeking to divert attention from new pups nearby. I avoided that section of the park for the couple of weeks that the coyote was around. One of the more fun animals I encountered was a herd of goats brought in by the park conservatory to help naturally clear out some of the brush in overgrown areas. I also once saw a turtle from the pond had crossed one of the pathways and was actively digging a hole to lay eggs. My client and I stopped for a few minutes to watch that miraculous event. The park in the middle of the city has been a beautiful microcosm of nearby nature for us city dwellers, allowing for lots of object lessons and metaphor" (personal communication, May 10, 2022).

Sometimes, these object lessons are as instructive for the therapist as they are for the client, as shown by the animal encounter story below.

• • • • •

Shantay is telling me about her summer plans when an energetic dog comes bounding over toward us. In the distance, we hear a voice shouting, "Max! Get back here!"

Now, I have been bitten by a dog before—as a result, seeing a dog off-leash still scares me. Knowing in that moment that I am not my best self, I stand still and take a few deep breaths as the dog charges at me, watching Shantay closely all the while.

To my surprise, she leans down and says, ever so quietly and gently, "Come here, Max. Aren't you a cutie? Here, boy!" Max dances around us and makes his way over to Shantay, who carefully pets his head before gently taking hold of his collar.

I comment, "Wow, Shantay, you're so good with him. Do you think we can get him back to his person?" By this time, a lady emerges on the trail, holding a leash and looking apologetic. Extremely grateful for us bringing him back to her, she puts on his collar and apologizes to us—they just got Max recently, and everyone is still adjusting.

We continue our walk in silence for a minute, composing ourselves after the disruption. When I look over at Shantay, I see that familiar little tear on her cheek. I ask, "What's on your mind?"

Shantay quietly answers, "That dog was so cute." Another pause, a big sigh, and she adds, "My bio mom's name is Maxine." A few more tears fall, and I wait for her to work through this emotional experience, just handing her a few tissues. Eventually, I respond, "Wow. What a coincidence. What did that mean to you to have Max the dog come over to you?"

"Well, it made me think that she is also trying to get to me," Shantay admits. "I never thought about that. I mean, I am always thinking about how I can get to her. The puppy was so sweet and jumpy—I liked feeling like it was a sign from my mom, or like maybe she was here in Max the dog." She takes a deep breath.

"It was kind of comforting," I suggest, and she nods. "I also noticed how brave you were. You are really good with dogs! You got right in there and knew instinctively what to do. I was a little scared, but I felt safe with your skills."

Shantay looks up in surprise and gives me a big warm smile with a little extra sparkle in her eyes. Then she surprises me by saying, "My mom has suggested that maybe we should adopt a dog. I was scared that if we did, and it didn't fit in, then we'd have to give it back to the shelter."

Before I have a chance to reflect that loaded thought back to Shantay, she adds, "But you know what? I think I've just changed my mind! I think it'd be great to adopt a dog!"

I say, "So you think you might be ready to let in a little something to love now? What's that like for you?"

She answers, "It feels really good. Like I know my bio mom will always be a part of me. And I can also love more and enjoy the good things."

This experience with Shantay was very powerful for both of us. When I first met Shantay, she was hurt, demoralized, and insecure, but when I saw her with Max the dog, I got to see a Shantay who was confident, able to take charge, and open to surprise encounters that some of her peers (or even a therapist) might find intimidating. The experience put us on the same footing, making us partners in problem-solving, and Shantay clearly felt well-deserved pride in having "protected" me. I felt so lucky to be outside where I could see this very different side of her. As a walk and talk therapist, the opportunities to get to know your client are unlimited.

Before moving on, I would like to note that if you have animal fears or concerns, please address those on your own before venturing out. Just as I have had to deal with my own "little t" trauma of the dog bite, I encourage you to do your own preparation and self-care. Also, please be compassionate with both your clients and yourself if animal encounters provide new information. If you've never seen a snake in your life, it's possible that you might get startled if you come across one on a trail. If this happens, take a deep breath and use this as a teaching moment for all who are present. We therapists are only human, with our own fears, anxieties, and stressors. The way we demonstrate how to handle these situations can be super powerful during a therapy session.

WHAT DO YOU DO ABOUT BILLING, SCHEDULING, AND OTHER PAPERWORK WHILE OUTSIDE?

Maybe it's just me, but something felt weird when my first few clients handed me cash in the parking lot. (A check felt only a drop more respectable.) After a bit of research, I opted for a credit card account that lets me take all payments electronically and added a permission form to my initial intake paperwork to allow use of credit cards. Now, I run cards after each session in the privacy of my home office. It feels safer, more ethical, and less cumbersome to keep billing and paperwork completely separate from the therapeutic interactions.

HOW DO YOU DECIDE HOW MANY WALK AND TALK SESSIONS TO DO EACH DAY OR WEEK?

This answer takes us back to the therapeutic frame. The main thing to consider in making your walk and talk schedule is how you can provide a positive and sustainable setup for your practice. Remembering that this form of therapy draws on your physical, mental, and emotional energy all at the same time, give some thought to what might be doable for you at first, and try some mock sessions with friends to see how much walk and talk you can handle each day.

I suggest beginning with one morning walk and one afternoon walk per week. Some beginning walk and talk therapists schedule their last appointment of the day as a walk; this way, there's no pressure to return to their office on time. Once you get the hang of this new format, you'll likely begin to feel energized (rather than drained) by your outdoor sessions. If you feel inspired to add more walking appointments, take it slowly. Maybe offer an additional morning walk and talk session at first, and if that feels good, add one more afternoon session for a total of four for the day. I've learned that I max out at five walking appointments in one day, and even that many is rare for me. Most days I'll see up to four clients outdoors, and that is after years of practice and building capacity. Remember, breaks are an important part of recharging, as is food and water—and even bathroom breaks! It's perfectly fine to go back for an office session between walk and talk meetings, or to follow a day of walk and talk with a day in the office. Your capacity may change over time, but a little trial and error will help you find your sweet spot.

> As you consider this new working lifestyle, take your own biology into account. If your office isn't in close enough proximity to take a bathroom break between sessions, consider whether park bathrooms or nearby public restrooms will be available to you. (Be sure to pay attention to whether facilities are closed at certain times of year, particularly winter.) As you become accustomed to your walk and talk practice, you'll start to notice your body's specific "routine" and can plan your schedule in a way that accommodates it.

When scheduling clients for walk and talk, it's second nature to consider their needs above your own. However, you'll want to offer a time and place that works for *you*; after all, you wouldn't relocate your office if a client said the drive was too far. If it's difficult for them to accommodate your schedule, I advise thinking seriously about how flexible you want to be. I have met clients at new parks or unusual times (7:00 a.m., yawn!) when I am able to, but I only do it if it works for me *and* I am happy to do it.

The reason for this is consistency—a very important factor for both the client and the therapist. This is something I learned the hard way when I relocated a client session following a full month of meeting at the same park in the same weekly time slot. The new place I recommended was very familiar to me, but my client did not know of the park. No problem—I told her I would send her the address. However, on our usual day and time, I sat waiting in the parking lot for the entire session, and the client did not show up. I tried texting, calling, and emailing, not only that afternoon but for several days afterward. No response. To this day, I still don't know what happened. Here are some options I've thought of:

1. The address was wrong, and her "smart" phone sent her to the wrong place.

2. She forgot and went to the original park.

3. There was something going on with her personally. Let's just say that this client was generally disorganized, overwhelmed, and upset about a number of things in her life. Changing to a different location might have just been one too many things for her to handle.

Long story short, I lost her as a client. While I admit this is an unusually drastic outcome to a one-time mix-up, it did reinforce my commitment to being consistent. There is something magical for clients about routine. People's lives are often in turmoil when they seek therapy—they are facing transitions, hardships, and mental health issues, which can include disorganized thinking or difficulty planning. As therapists, our clients count on us to provide a sense of stability.

Now, if a client requests a change to another location that works better for them, I am open to discussing it. Just remember to communicate clearly, and definitely check in the day before to confirm the plan.

HOW DO YOU HANDLE DOCUMENTATION OF YOUR WALK AND TALK SESSION?

I am often asked, "How do you take notes during a session?" The short answer is that I don't. Interestingly, I tend to remember walking sessions better that way. I've found that I can easily associate parts of the conversation with the scene where they happened or the conditions we encountered along the way.

· · · · ·

I meet up with Joanie on a very hot day in late summer. I show up to the trail with my arsenal of gear: big straw hat, water bottle, and sunscreen spackled over my face, neck, and shoulders. In the car, I have a cooler packed with extra water, ice packs, deodorant, more sunscreen, electrolyte tablets, and a cool towel. We take a second to compare supplies, laughing at how accustomed we've become to walk and talk sessions in the summertime. Joanie is also prepared with extra water and a small bowl for Pepper to drink from. As we retreat to the cool shade of the wooded trail, she starts right in.

"You know how I told you about that woman I met? Well, we are going to get together tomorrow night after work. I can't believe it. I'm kind of flipping out. I don't even know what to do!" She chatters eagerly about her simultaneous excitement and anxiety, though by the time we begin our uphill climb, the anxiety has taken over. "How do I greet her? What should we talk about? What if it becomes awkward, or there is a really long pause? How about if I get overwhelmed or tired out by her energy?"

Once we reach the top of the hill, we take some deep breaths, followed by deep swallows of our water, Pepper included. When we're finally refreshed enough to look out over the view, I say, "You can probably come up with a coping skill for each of the challenges you just listed. Think of it like the supplies I have back in the car."

She instantly gets the idea. "Okay, my coping skills for this conversation can be that I'll have a few ideas for conversation prepared. Like bringing water on a hot hike." I nod, coaxing her on. "The dog bowl can be like . . ." She thinks. ". . . the conversation lull. I can just wait and take a deep wide breath that will help me feel calm, rather than trying to compensate with some goofy story." Now she's on a roll. "If I get tired by her energy, I'll tell her that I am really tired because I had a long day. That's sort of like how the electrolyte tablets give you a boost, so you can get home. And ending the date can be like the cool towel you brought! I can end it well by just saying I had a good time, but I can't stay out late because I have to get an early start the next day."

As we make our way to the end of the trail, Joanie asks if we can do that mindfulness exercise that we started with nearly a year ago. We have practiced it so much by now that it's not really an exercise anymore—she finds real peace in this technique. Putting one hand on her stomach and one on her chest, Joanie takes a deep breath in and a long exhale out, then adds her mantra: "I've got this. It's okay to be me, and I accept myself the way I am. I am here."

Back at my home office, I sit down with a large glass of ice water and begin to fill in my client notes. I close my eyes for ten seconds and picture the walk that I took with Joanie. I remember how when we walked over the bridge in the park, she was talking about going on the date that she was nervous about. (Easy to associate anxiety with a bridge). We went on past the playground (there were kids laughing and playing), and she talked about the purpose of going on the date: to get to know someone and have fun. We next climbed the hill and discussed the challenges that she may face with navigating social situations. Toward the end of the walk, we brainstormed some coping strategies for the event. This included both familiar and new ideas. Lastly, a few minutes before we ended, we paused by the stream and watched the ducks splash in the water. Here we focused on how calming it can be to live in the present, rather than always looking forward in anxious anticipation.

It's amazing how these sensory cues make for quick and accurate post-session note-taking. There's just one catch: It's essential to do it as soon as possible after seeing the client, before the memories fade or are replaced by too many other sessions. While I know documentation is nobody's favorite part of therapy or social work, it is also a valuable piece of our job. The sooner you write, the sooner it's done, and you can move on to the next session.

HOW DO YOU BILL INSURANCE? IS THERE A CODE FOR WALK AND TALK? DO YOU NEED A BRICK-AND-MORTAR OFFICE?

Insurance. The billable therapy session. Managed care. *Grrrr.*

I won't get on a soapbox about the health care inequity problem that affects so many clients. I will, however, focus on the loaded question of what to do with your session invoice or receipt. At the time of this book's publication, there are no codes for walk and talk therapy sessions, so I continue to use the usual CPT codes. If you are an in-network provider, it would be reasonable for you to call the insurance companies that you are paneled on to find out if they have a separate code for walk and talk (or simply ask them how to code for a walk and talk session). Most likely, though, they won't have a hard-and-fast answer for you—in that case, you should simply code as a regular session. If you have an office that you will be leaving from and returning to, that in-office code may be used in some instances. Another possibility is to use the code for a community visit, though this, too, may warrant a phone call to the insurance company to find out if therapy can be done in a community setting; the location code or modifier may reflect that. If you pursue this option, I'd recommend starting by asking the company, "What entails a community visit? And can therapy be done in a community setting?"

If you are out of network with insurance, please advise your client of this from the get-go and recommend that they call their insurance company ahead of time to find out about their coverage for walk and talk. Please make sure that they understand when they are responsible for their own insurance paperwork.

If you have the flexibility to accept private pay, please be kind to your clients and offer any help or advice you can. Insurance companies and plans are difficult to navigate, and having been paneled in the past, I know how great an advantage it is to understand the system. This experience has helped me coach clients through navigating their own reimbursement paperwork. Every once in a while, a client with strong advocacy skills has been able to negotiate with their insurance company to make an exception that allows coverage for walk and talk sessions. This usually has to do with the client's specific diagnosis as well as proof that they were unsuccessful in traditional office settings.

In closing, I think I might get up on the soapbox for a moment to advocate for clients: Insurance companies, please accept walk and talk as a valid and appropriate therapeutic intervention and make a code that providers can easily use to allow clients reimbursement. If anyone reading this works in the behavioral health insurance industry, now is the time to take action. (I'm ready to support the movement—just call me!)

HOW DO YOU HANDLE A MENTAL HEALTH CRISIS AND CONTINUE TO MOVE FORWARD AFTER ONE HAPPENS?

Let's say you are walking with a client and they get really angry. Maybe they are telling you how they were wronged at work or in a relationship. Maybe the client has uncovered a realization, a memory, or an emotional wound during your session. As a therapist, you are always aware of how a client is reacting, but as a walking therapist, you witness even more of their body language. You notice them acting up, raising their voice, crying, or pounding one fist into the other palm.

First of all, you need to assess the situation. Are they safe? Are you safe? If the answer is no, stop the walk and ask them what they need. If you determine you need reinforcement, please inform your client that you'll be calling 911 to help both of you handle this crisis. Make sure you get your client to a safe place and implement all of your skills to help them calm down. Keep yourself calm by practicing (and demonstrating) slower, deeper breaths. Offer water, a jacket if they're cold, and any other comforts that are appropriate. Call a colleague if one is available. Just as office mates help each other during crises at work, it's okay to ask your fellow therapists for support.

Remember to stay with your client in crisis. If you have another appointment after, inform your next client that you'll need to reschedule. (And trust that the next client will understand, since you would provide them the same amount of time and care if they were in distress.)

Do *not* attempt to drive your client anywhere. Getting in the car with them could be a liability on your part, as well as a safety concern. If they need to go to the hospital or be in someone else's care after the session ends, offer to make that call together or even for your client.

As a social worker, I have handled emergencies of this sort in the office, and always followed through to the end—in other words, until I know that my client is in safe hands. That commitment has not changed since switching to walking therapy. I still want to know my clients are safe after a crisis and that I did the best I could to care for them.

HOW DO YOU HANDLE A STRANGER WHO WITNESSES YOUR CLIENT'S MENTAL HEALTH CRISIS?

What if a mental health crisis were to happen while walking, and you pass by people you either know or do not know? Number one, you are looking out for your client's safety. If there is no need to disclose your therapist-client relationship, then do not tell others in the park about that status. However, as we discussed in chapter 12, you may need to disclose to the first responder that you are the client's therapist in order to keep the client safe. Again, confidentiality does not apply as usual when someone's personal safety is at risk.

A PLACE TO START YOUR JOURNEY

I hope these answers provided resolution to some of your specific questions, or at least pointed you in the right direction. As I've said many times in this book, so much of growing in your practice is finding what works for your specific needs and those of your clients. Sometimes the simple answers don't suffice—that's why I encourage you to think for yourself and even question the way things have always been done. I also encourage you to find your own network of like-minded professionals to help you grow your walk and talk practice and create solutions for the challenges you encounter.

Chapter 15

The Future of Walk and Talk Therapy

I like to imagine that, about one hundred years ago, a group of psychiatrists worked together to plant a seed. From that seed, a discipline called psychotherapy took root. Each year, as it grew stronger, that tree grew branches, each one slightly different, reaching farther into the sky while sprouting fresh seeds that flew to all ends of the earth. New saplings grew from these seeds, some growing deep roots while others were short-lived or hybridized with other types of seeds. Meanwhile, the original tree continued to reach higher and expand its branches, drawing more and more people under its sheltering canopy. Today, the tree remains tall and strong—the foundation of our field, a helper and a healer that teaches us to grow, change, and expand, keeping what's good while shedding what's not.

When the field of psychotherapy began, it was one thing, but it has since evolved into many different disciplines and practices. Walk and talk therapy has shown the psychiatric field that there are more possibilities for healing and a wider landscape of access to therapy. We've seen this play out in the stories I've shared throughout this book:

- Joanie utilizing her anxious energy to find a grounded place where she can handle the issues that regularly challenge her.

- Taylor learning to connect her thoughts with her movement to rebuild her sense of self-empowerment.

- Jake finding a way to reach out for help to articulate the deep emotions connected with his loss.

- Shantay "getting into" herself and developing her own sense of identity amongst the many parts of her story.

Could these milestones have been reached without walking during the therapy session? Honestly, I think this question is too big—too generalized—to answer. As beginner therapists, we're taught to "start where the client's at." If walk and talk is what they signed up for, then that's exactly what they need. Every individual client is unique, but for some, the movement, the natural space, and the undoing of the power differential are essential to finding the comfort and confidence they need to do the work. Meeting outdoors and moving together sheds a layer of the "us versus them" dynamic that can obstruct the productiveness of the therapeutic relationship.

One of the most important things that walk and talk can do is get us thinking about how the range of treatment approaches must be broadened. Thousands, if not millions, of people are living with mental illness; expanding their options for treatment is, in my view, part of our responsibility as health care providers. The world is always changing, and we need to be able to change with it. What if we simply included questions in our intake about a client's activity level and their relationship to nature? Imagine what you could learn about their health and self-care, their memories and past experiences, their fears and hopes and sources of inspiration. Living on this planet has given all of us a relationship with nature and with our bodies—exploring and expanding those relationships can yield tremendous insight for their healing.

With that in mind, I hope you'll use the ideas in this book as a springboard for your own creative version of walk and talk therapy. Even if you're not feeling ready to go outside with clients, consider the potential for movement in therapy, as well as the restorative power of the natural world. While walk and talk is not the sole cure for mental health problems, adding nature and movement to your already existing therapeutic toolbox can help clients feel less alone and more empowered. Therapists come and go, but nature and movement will always be available to soothe, heal, and empower.

On an advocacy level, I encourage you to approach insurance companies for better coverage of outdoor sessions. Let's rally together for a new location code to recognize walk and talk therapy as a valid alternative treatment. It should be possible to integrate walk and talk into programs at mental health clinics, school counseling sessions, and intensive outpatient programs.

I also urge higher learning institutions to include classes, books, research groups, and trainings in ecotherapy. In my view, we need certifications for the growing variety of approaches and techniques to be reliably effective. We need more data about the efficacy of walk and talk therapy—ideally, a group of academics and practicing therapists collaborating to create an online database of walk and talk practitioners, for both research and client access. In the meantime, if you are considering entering the field, I encourage you to take a close look at ecotherapy classes or movement-based practices. The field is only growing, and as we've seen, it's constantly giving us reasons to learn more about the power of nature and movement in healing our mental health.

66 *Live in each season
as it passes; breathe the air,
drink the drink, taste the fruit,
and resign yourself to the
influence of the earth.* **99**

—Henry David Thoreau

Conclusion

In the autumn, when it's getting cold outside and warm inside, I try to find ways to embrace the season. For me, that starts in my kitchen, trading slow cooker recipes with my friends that will keep our families happy and warm. It's rare that any of us follow the directions exactly as they're written. Instead, we test, tinker, and share with each other what worked for us and what didn't. In the end, we each find the version that satisfies our family and makes us want to come back for more.

This is how I think about the work that has been done over generations of walking therapy. Each bit of information is like a key ingredient in the recipe, while each individual practice yields new insights for how to apply it. In closing, I offer you my own recipe for a productive walk and talk practice:

1. Start with a hearty base of therapy training—any approach will do.

2. Next, add some flavorful fresh ingredients: a natural setting with plenty of green space, fresh air, and a source of water. Add additional techniques and approaches to taste: a little CBT, some psychodynamic psychotherapy, a dash of DBT—whatever promises to suit the palate of you and your client.

3. Keep the heat source flowing through breath work and mindfulness.

4. Stir in movement with regular, rhythmic twists and turns.

5. Lastly, this is not a secret recipe. Sharing will bring out the hidden flavors and unexpected nutrients that can offer even greater warmth and comfort to those you serve.

The journey of the walk and talk practice that I began ten years ago is one that I continue to travel, always learning and gathering new information along the way. I wish you well on your own journey as you continue to grow and learn.

Thank you to the researchers, writers, and publishers who have contributed to the work so far. Because of you, there are therapists practicing outdoors all over the world!

And thank you for reading this book. May we all remain open to fresh possibilities, try new things, and keep on moving!

Recommended Readings

Charbonneau, T. (2016). *Get out! A narrative inquiry with four therapists who practice walk and talk therapy* [Unpublished doctoral dissertation]. University of Calgary.

Crowe Clark, D. (2019). *Adult clients' experience of walk-and-talk therapy* [Doctoral dissertation, Walden University]. https://scholarworks.waldenu.edu/cgi/viewcontent .cgi?article=8058&context=dissertations

Doucette, P. A. (2004). Walk and talk: An intervention for behaviorally challenged youths. *Adolescence, 39*(154), 373–388.

Hays, K. F. (1999). *Working it out: Using exercise in psychotherapy*. American Psychological Association.

Jordan, M. (2013). *Taking therapy outside—A narrative inquiry into counselling and psychotherapy in outdoor natural spaces* [Doctoral dissertation, University of Brighton]. https://cris .brighton.ac.uk/ws/portalfiles/portal/4755959/Final+2014+pdf+PHD+.pdf

Jordan, M. (2014). Moving beyond counselling and psychotherapy as it currently is—taking therapy outside. *European Journal of Psychotherapy & Counselling, 16(*4), 361–375. https:// doi.org/10.1080/13642537.2014.956773

Jordan, M. (2014). *Nature and therapy: Understanding counselling and psychotherapy in outdoor spaces.* Routledge.

Jordan, M., & Marshall, H. (2010). Taking counselling and psychotherapy outside: Destruction or enrichment of the therapeutic frame? *European Journal of Psychotherapy & Counselling, 12*(4), 345–359. https://doi.org/10.1080/13642537.2010.530105

King, B. (2015). *The shared experiences of counselors who practice in natural environments* [Doctoral dissertation, University of New Orleans]. http://scholarworks.uno.edu/cgi /viewcontent.cgi?article=3121&context=td

McKinney, B. (2011). *Therapist's perceptions of walk and talk therapy: A grounded study* [Doctoral dissertation, University of New Orleans]. http://scholarworks.uno.edu/cgi/viewcontent .cgi?article=2381&context=td

Revell, S. (2017). Walk and talk therapy: Potential client perceptions. *Scope (Health & Wellbeing), 2*, 24–34.

Revell, S., Duncan, E., & Cooper, M. (2014). Helpful aspects of outdoor therapy experiences: An online preliminary investigation. *Counselling and Psychotherapy Research, 14*(4), 281–287. https://doi.org/10.1080/14733145.2013.818159

Revell, S., & McLeod, J. (2016). Experiences of therapists who integrate walk and talk into their professional practice. *Counselling and Psychotherapy Research, 16*, 35–43. https://doi.org/10.1002/capr.12042

Revell, S., & McLeod, J. (2017). Therapists' experience of walk and talk therapy: A descriptive phenomenological study. *European Journal of Psychotherapy & Counselling, 19*(3), 267–289. https://doi.org/10.1080/13642537.2017.1348377

References

American Horticultural Therapy Association. (2022). *History of horticultural therapy.* https://www .ahta.org/index.php?option=com_content&view=article&id=85:history-of-horticultural -therapy&catid=20:site-content

Barton, J., & Pretty, J. (2010). What is the best dose of nature and green exercise for improving mental health? A multi-study analysis. *Environmental Science & Technology*, 44(10), 3947– 3955. https://doi.org/10.1021/es903183r

Berger, R. (2009). Being in nature: An innovative framework for incorporating nature in therapy with older adults. *Journal of Holistic Nursing*, 27(1), 45–50. https://doi.org /10.1177/0898010108323010

Berger, R., & McLeod, J. (2006). Incorporating nature into therapy: A framework for practice. *Journal of Systemic Therapies*, 25(2), 80–94. https://doi.org/10.1521/jsyt.2006.25.2.80

Berman, M. G., Kross, E., Krpan, K. M., Askren, M. K., Burson, A., Deldin, P. J., Kaplan, S., Sherdell, L., Gotlib, I. H., & Jonides, J. (2012). Interacting with nature improves cognition and affect for individuals with depression. *Journal of Affective Disorders*, 140(3), 300–305. https://doi.org/10.1016/j.jad.2012.03.012

Buzzell, L., & Chalquist, C. (Eds.). (2009). *Ecotherapy: Healing with nature in mind.* Counterpoint.

Chiu, A. (2020, November 13). Teletherapy is helping Americans get through the pandemic. What happens afterward? *The Washington Post.* https://www.washingtonpost.com/lifestyle /wellness/telehealth-teletherapy-mental-health-covid/2020/11/12/fdda8776-242c-11eb -952e-0c475972cfc0_story.html

Cooley, S. J., Jones, C. R., Kurtz, A., & Robertson, N. (2020). Into the wild: A meta-synthesis of talking therapy in natural outdoor spaces. *Journal Clinical Psychology Review*, 77, Article 101841. https://doi.org/10.1016/j.cpr.2020.101841

Fraga, J. (2020, November 14). Pandemic spurs boom in outdoor therapy sessions, allowing in-person treatment. *The Washington Post.* https://www.washingtonpost.com/health /therapists-outdoor-meetings/2020/11/13/a9e99308-13ad-11eb-ad6f-36c93e6e94fb_story .html

Fromm, E. (1973). *The anatomy of human destructiveness.* Holt, Rinehart and Winston.

Gladwell, V. F., Brown, D. K., Woods, C., Sandercock, G. R., & Barton, J. L. (2013). The great outdoors: How a green exercise environment can benefit all. *Extreme Physiology & Medicine*, 2, Article 3. https://doi.org/10.1186/2046-7648-2-3

Hunter, M. R., Gillespie, B. W., & Chen, S. Y. P. (2019). Urban nature experiences reduce stress in the context of daily life based on salivary biomarkers. *Frontiers in Psychology, 10*, Article 722. https://doi.org/10.3389/fpsyg.2019.00722

Jordan, M. (2014). *Nature and therapy: Understanding counselling and psychotherapy in outdoor spaces.* Routledge.

Jordan, M., & Marshall, H. (2010). Taking counselling and psychotherapy outside: Destruction or enrichment of the therapeutic frame? *European Journal of Psychotherapy and Counselling, 12*(4), 345–359. https://doi.org/10.1080/13642537.2010.530105

Kostrubala, T. (1976). *The joy of running.* Lippincott.

The Lancet Infectious Diseases. (2020). The intersection of COVID-19 and mental health. *The Lancet: Infectious Diseases, 20*(11), 1217. https://doi.org/10.1016/S1473-3099(20)30797-0

Moss, A., & Greene, N. (2021, May/June). Facing the waves: Therapy in the surf circle. *Psychotherapy Networker.* https://www.psychotherapynetworker.org/magazine/article/2542/facing-the-waves

Nagoski, E., & Nagoski, A. (2019). *Burnout: The secret to unlocking the stress cycle.* Ballantine Books.

Olszewska-Guizzo, A., Fogel, A., Escoffier, N., Sia, A., Nakazawa, K., Kumagai, A., Dan, I., & Ho, R. (2022). Therapeutic garden with contemplative features induces desirable changes in mood and brain activity in depressed adults. *Frontiers in Psychiatry, 13*, Article 757056. https://doi.org/10.3389/fpsyt.2022.757056

Paquette, J. (2020). *Awestruck: How embracing wonder can make you happier, healthier, and more connected.* Shambhala.

Rassovsky, Y., & Alfassi, T. (2019). Attention improves during physical exercise in individuals with ADHD. *Frontiers in Psychology, 9*, Article 2747.

Rutgers School of Environmental and Biological Sciences. (2022). *What is horticultural therapy?* Horticulture Therapy Program. https://plantbiology.rutgers.edu/hort-therapy/whatis.html

Santostefano, S. (2008). The sense of self inside and environments outside: How the two grow together and become one in healthy psychological development. *Psychoanalytic Dialogues, 18*(4), 513–535. https://doi.org/10.1080/10481880802198384

Sapolsky, R. M. (2004). *Why zebras don't get ulcers.* Henry Holt and Company.

Scheinfeld, D. E., Rochlen, A. B., & Buser, S. J. (2011). Adventure therapy: A supplementary group therapy approach for men. *Psychology of Men & Masculinity, 12*(2), 188–194. https://doi.org/10.1037/a0022041

Stellar, J. E., John-Henderson, N., Anderson, C. L., Gordon, A. M., McNeil, G. D., & Keltner, D. (2015). Positive affect and markers of inflammation: Discrete positive emotions predict lower levels of inflammatory cytokines. *Emotion, 15*(2), 129–133. https://doi.org/10.1037/emo0000033

van der Kolk, B. (2014). *The body keeps the score: Brain, mind, and body in the healing of trauma.* Penguin.

Waddell, M. (1992). *Owl babies.* Candlewick.

Williams, F. (2017). *The nature fix: Why nature makes us happier, healthier, and more creative.* W. W. Norton.

Wilson, E. O. (1984). *Biophilia: The human bond with other species.* Harvard University Press.

Wilson, E. O. (1993). Biophilia and the conservation ethic. In S. R. Kellert & E. O. Wilson (Eds.), *The biophilia hypothesis* (pp. 31–41). Shearwater.

Acknowledgments

I would, first of all, like to thank Chelsea Thompson, my brilliant editor! As a first-time author, I am extremely grateful for Chelsea's guidance, attention to detail, and partnership. Thank you to Jenessa Jackson, Kate Sample, Kayla Church, and the PESI Publishing team for their hard work, availability, and faith in this innovative topic. Way to go, PESI and Psychotherapy Networker, for the brave and determined work that you do for our field.

Thank you to my family. My husband, Josh, for believing in me, being the first to read my manuscript, and walking together with me through this adventure called life. Thank you to our children, Jacob, Shoshanna, and Jonah. You were patient while I got lost in writing, lost track of time, and set the smoke detector off nightly while not paying attention to dinner. Thank you for listening to me talk about my book and for helping me relieve stress with dance parties in the kitchen! You guys are the absolute best, and I love you to the moon and back.

Thank you to my parents for teaching me everything and for being so excited for and supportive of me while I wrote this book. I am grateful that you have shown such interest in my professional life. I love our exchange of thoughts. Thank you to my sister, Wendy, for being my confidant, supporter, and best friend. Thank you to all my nieces and nephews, who inspire me every day to think outside the box.

Thank you to JJ for making me write this book. I appreciate that much-needed push and all the love and writing wisdom you share. Thank you to Anne, friend for life, for always being so positive and for making me laugh! Lisa, thank you for being my MSW buddy; if we hadn't shared our books, I never could have shared this one. Thank you to Karen for helping me find my voice and the meaning in sharing my story.

To my running buddies, Jenny, Lili, Jocelyn, and Tanya. We have accomplished more than marathons. We have worked through many personal defining moments. You've kept my feet moving, my thoughts flowing, and my heart laughing!

To the walking cheer committee, Michelle and Jane. Thank you for always asking, being there, and listening to me talk every week about this book. You are such amazing friends, and I can't thank you enough for being with me on this pursuit and for raising my kids!

To the Positive Strides team, I can't imagine doing any of this without you. You are the dream team—rock-solid, amazing clinicians and coworkers. Jennifer and Aliza, thank you for your reassurance and for holding me accountable. The writing memes, the long talks, and the dinners have led me to this accomplishment. Thank you to the PS moms—for many days, I wrote thinking you may be the only ones to read this book.

Thank you to all the walk and talk therapists I have met over the years. Whether you were already on a roll or learning to walk the walk, I truly admire you. I want to especially thank Denice Crowe Clark, whom I consider to be the voice of reason in walk and talk therapy. Your calm demeanor, care, and detailed research has helped make the field what it is today. I thank all the walk and talk therapists who graciously contributed to this book. You all are so amazing, generous, and excited about your work outdoors. I hope we continue to work together and inspire one another to move forward on our paths.

Lastly, I want to thank my clients. I am grateful for your courageous steps to move therapy outdoors. Your confidence in me is the ultimate gift. I am the lucky one to be walking with you on your therapeutic journey.